Classical Music

An Introduction

Classical Music

An Introduction

MICHAEL SWIFT

CHARTWELL
BOOKS, INC.

First published in 2010 by

CHARTWELL BOOKS, INC.
A Division of
BOOK SALES, INC.
276 Fifth Avenue Suite 206
New York, New York 10001

ISBN 13: 978-0-7858-2730-6

Project manager: Rodney Burbeck

Designed by: Angela Ball and Dave Ball at daviball@sky.com

All Internet site information provided was correct when provided by
the Author. The Publisher can accept no responsibility for this
information becoming incorrect.

Printed and bound in China

Acknowledgements:
Thanks to Simon Clay for the still photography.

The quote by *Hildegard von Bingen* (page 23) is taken from *Scivias*,
translated by Columba Hart and Jane Bishop [New York: Paulist
Press, 1990]

CONTENTS

INTRODUCTION

We live in an age surrounded by music, be it the advertising jingle, the mobile phone ring–tone, the incidental themes in television or cinema, or the Muzak that provides the backdrop whilst on hold when dialing a call center. Much of this music is derived from the great classics, and many people who would not normally recognize themselves as connoisseurs of the classical repertoire discover a love of the works of composers such as Handel, Bach, Mozart and Beethoven through these influences. Despite this familiarity, however, some people can be intimidated by the apparent complexity and variety of classical music and are reluctant to explore further the great music bequeathed to us over the past millennium.

The history of classical music is very much the history of western civilization, a reflection of the ages in which the individual composers lived and of the instruments that they could call upon. From the Gregorian chant of the medieval church, through Vivaldi's *Four Seasons*, Handel's *Messiah*, Tchaikovsky's *1812 Overture* and Beethoven's *Ninth Symphony*, with its *Ode to Joy*, to Elgar's *Pomp and Circumstance Marches*, the great pieces of classical music both reflect the tone of the eras in which they were composed and help to define them for a modern audience.

For individuals and nations alike, the great classical pieces classify important stages of life. Mendelssohn's

Above: The Coronation of Queen Victoria in Westminster Abbey, 1838

Wedding March and the Third Movement of Chopin's Piano Sonata No. 2, the *Funeral March*, are amongst the most familiar to many of us–whilst on great state occasions striking anthems underscore events, as with Handel's *Zadok the Priest*, which is played at the Coronation of British monarchs. More recently, few who heard the playing of Samuel Barber's *Adagio for Strings* conducted by the American Leonard Slatkin at the Last Night of the Proms at London's Royal Albert Hall on September 15, 2001–four days after the terrorist attacks on New York and the Pentagon–will ever forget the emotional impact of this superb piece of music at that highly charged time.

The history of classical music can be divided into distinct

phases—Early and Renaissance, Baroque, Classical, Romantic and Modern—with notable composers working in each of these periods, and with familiar tunes appearing throughout. The earlier periods tended, inevitably, to be dominated by music produced for use by the church—with the Reformation and the rise of increasingly secular societies, increasing

Above: French Horn quartet in performance dress, rehearse before a concert

Top right: Military band at the "Trooping the Colour" ceremony in London

Pages 10–11: The "Last Night of the Proms" at London's Royal Albert Hall

emphasis was given to music as a form of entertainment.

Fostered by the great courts and patrons of the Renaissance and Baroque periods, and dominated by the small–scale ensembles capable of playing the chamber music required, music increasingly became a source of entertainment for paying audiences. Concerts and other musical programs were staged in purpose–built concert halls, for example, together with the growth of distinct forms of music—ballet and opera—that offered spectacle, but at a price.

In many respects the modern audience is spoilt; there is still great music being composed, much of it experimental and making use of new techniques and equipment, whilst the great store of historic music is also available through CDs and downloads. The modern audience can now, perhaps as never before, explore fully the range of tone and instruments that have helped to shape the western traditional of classical music. With pioneers like the conductors David Munrow and John Eliot Gardiner, it is now recognized that it is possible to play pieces of Baroque music, for example, on authentic instruments, providing the audience with a true feel for the intimate nature of this type of music.

In a book of this nature, it is only possible to provide the briefest overview of the development of classical music. Each of the major phases of classical music is examined and a history of some of the major composers for each period is given. Briefer details of other significant composers for each period are also provided. Further information on each of these periods and composers is well worth tracking down, and the section on further reading and websites will be useful. The information here only scratches the surface of the history and the world of classical music, but it is a good starting point for your research. The accompanying CD will give a flavor of the music from each of the eras described in the text: it is designed very much to whet the appetite in the hope that you will like what you hear and want to explore further the music and composers written about in these pages.

TIMELINE

590–604 Development of Gregorian chant

695 Development of organum, an early form of counterpoint

1000 Musical notation improved by Guido d'Arrezo

1050 Polyphonic singing replaces Gregorian chant; harp arrives in Europe; time values given to musical notation

1090 First Crusade; capture of Jerusalem

1125 Beginning of troubadour music in France

1136 Hildegard elected head of the Benedictine convent of Bingen in Germany

1163 Construction begins on the cathedral of Notre Dame in Paris

1200 Cymbals introduced as musical instruments

1325 Organ pedals come into use; first polyphonic Mass still extant, the *Tournai Mass* composed

1340 Guillaume de Machaut, who undertook the copying of complete musical works, becomes residentiary canon of Rheims in France

1347 Black Death reaches Europe, massive population loss

1360 Start of the development of the clavichord and cembalo

1437 John Dunstable develops counterpoint in musical composition

1453 Fall of Constantinople

1454 Gutenberg invents the printing press

1465 First printed music

1490 Ballet begins at Italian courts

1492 Columbus's first voyage to the New World

1499 University of Oxford institutes degrees in music

1505 Birth of Tallis

1509 Henry VIII comes to the throne in England

1516 Engraving of music on plates used for the first time in Italy

1517 Martin Luther's 95 Theses; the start of the Protestant Reformation

1536 First song book with lute accompaniment printed in Spain

1542 Birth of Byrd

1553 The violin in its present form begins to develop

1567 Birth of Monteverdi

1570 Earliest known music festival, to honour St Cecilia, is held in Normandy

1573 First meeting of the Florentine Camerata

1580 English folk tune *Greensleeves* mentioned for the first time

1585 Giovanni Gabrieli appointed chapel master at St Mark's in Venice; death of Tallis

1600 Harps first added to orchestras; the recorder (also known as flute–a–bec) becomes popular in England

1606 First open air operas in Rome

1616 Collegium Musicum founded at Prague

1623 Death of Byrd

1637 Birth of Buxtehude; Teatro San Cassiano, first public opera house, opens in Venice, sponsored by the Tron family

1643 Death of Monteverdi

1644 Antonio Stradivari, Italian violin maker, born

1648 Aria and recitative become two distinct entities in opera

1650 Nicolo Amati perfects the modern violin in Cremona, Italy; beginning of modern harmony; development of modulation; the overture as musical form emerges in two types, Italian and French

1652 The minuet comes into fashion at French court; the first opera house in Vienna opens

1653 Birth of Corelli

1659 Birth of Purcell

1660 Birth of Scarlatti

1664 French horn becomes an orchestral instrument

1669 Royal patent for founding Academie Royale des Operas granted in France to Pierre Perrin

1671 Paris Opera opens

1678 Birth of Vivaldi; first opera house in Germany opens in Hamburg

1685 Birth of Bach; birth of Handel

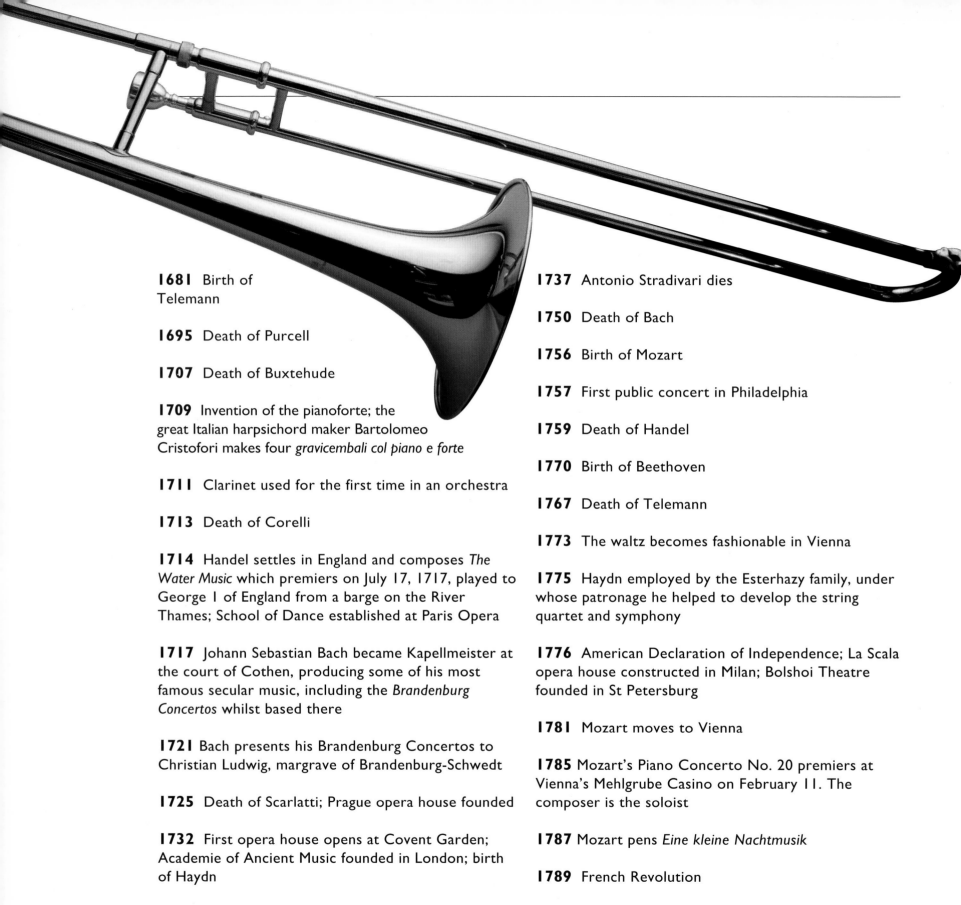

1681 Birth of Telemann

1695 Death of Purcell

1707 Death of Buxtehude

1709 Invention of the pianoforte; the great Italian harpsichord maker Bartolomeo Cristofori makes four *gravicembali col piano e forte*

1711 Clarinet used for the first time in an orchestra

1713 Death of Corelli

1714 Handel settles in England and composes *The Water Music* which premiers on July 17, 1717, played to George I of England from a barge on the River Thames; School of Dance established at Paris Opera

1717 Johann Sebastian Bach became Kapellmeister at the court of Cothen, producing some of his most famous secular music, including the *Brandenburg Concertos* whilst based there

1721 Bach presents his Brandenburg Concertos to Christian Ludwig, margrave of Brandenburg-Schwedt

1725 Death of Scarlatti; Prague opera house founded

1732 First opera house opens at Covent Garden; Academie of Ancient Music founded in London; birth of Haydn

1737 Antonio Stradivari dies

1750 Death of Bach

1756 Birth of Mozart

1757 First public concert in Philadelphia

1759 Death of Handel

1770 Birth of Beethoven

1767 Death of Telemann

1773 The waltz becomes fashionable in Vienna

1775 Haydn employed by the Esterhazy family, under whose patronage he helped to develop the string quartet and symphony

1776 American Declaration of Independence; La Scala opera house constructed in Milan; Bolshoi Theatre founded in St Petersburg

1781 Mozart moves to Vienna

1785 Mozart's Piano Concerto No. 20 premiers at Vienna's Mehlgrube Casino on February 11. The composer is the soloist

1787 Mozart pens *Eine kleine Nachtmusik*

1789 French Revolution

1791 Death of Mozart

1792 Birth of Rossini

1795 Paris Conservatoire de Musique founded

1797 Birth of Schubert

1798 Haydn finishes the *Missa in Angustiis*–commonly known as the "Lord Nelson Mass" to commemorate the admiral's victory at the Battle of the Nile

1799 Napoleon seizes power in France

1803 Birth of Berlioz

1804 Birth of Strauss (the Elder); Napoleon crowned emperor of France

1808 Beethoven completes Symphony No. 5–possibly the most famous piece of classical music ever written. It premiers in Vienna

1809 Death of Haydn; birth of Mendelssohn

1810 Birth of Chopin; birth of Schumann

1812 Napoleon's retreat from Moscow

1813 Birth of Verdi; birth of Wagner; London Philharmonic Society founded

1822 Royal Academy of Music, London, founded

1824 Birth of Bruckner; Schubert composes his "Death and the Maiden" string quartet. It will not be published until 1831, three years after his death

1825 Birth of Strauss (the Younger); opening of new Bolshoi Theatre building in St Petersburg to the design of Andrei Mikhailov

1827 Death of Beethoven

1828 Death of Schubert

1833 Birth of Brahms

1835 Tuba patented by Wilhelm Friedrich Wieprecht and Carl Moritz

1841 Birth of Dvořák

1842 New York Philharmonic Society founded by violinist Ureli C. Hill

1843 Birth of Grieg

1845 Birth of Fauré

1846 Adolphe Sax, the Belgian instrument maker, patents the saxophone

1847 Death of Mendelssohn; flute patented by Thomas Böhm

1849 Death of Chopin; death of Strauss (the Elder)

1854 Brahms composes his first Piano Trio. He would revise it in 1891

1856 Death of Schumann

1857 Birth of Elgar; Charles Halle founds the Halle concerts in Manchester, England

1858 Birth of Puccini

1859 Charles Darwin publishes his *On the Origin of Species*

1860 Birth of Mahler

1862 Birth of Debussy; birth of Delius

1864 Birth of Strauss (Richard)

1865 Birth of Sibelius

1868 Death of Rossini

1869 Death of Berlioz

1871 The Albert Hall, London, opens; Verdi's *Aïda* premiers at the Khedivial Opera House in Cairo on December 24, conducted by Giovanni Bottesini

1872 Birth of Vaughan Williams

1874 Birth of Holst; completion of new opera house in Paris

1875 The most popular opera in the world–Bizet's *Carmen*-premiers at the Paris Opéra–Comique on March 3 to almost universal critical disapproval!

1876 Bayreuth Festspielhaus opens with first complete performance of Wagner's *Ring des Nibelungen*

1877 Invention of the phonograph by Thomas Edison; Tchaikovsky's *Swan Lake* premiers at the Bolshoi.

1879 Birth of Respighi

1881 Boston Symphony Orchestra founded

1882 Berlin Philharmonic Orchestra founded

1883 Death of Wagner; Metropolitan Opera House, New York, opens; Royal College of Music, London, founded

1888 Koninklijk Concertgebouworkest founded; Rimsky-Korsakov finishes his symphonic suite *Scheherazade*

1890 The premiere of Tchaikovsky's *The Sleeping Beauty* takes place at the Mariinsky Theatre in St. Petersburg

1896 Death of Bruckner

1897 Death of Brahms

1899 Death of Strauss (the Younger)

1901 Death of Queen Victoria; death of Verdi

1904 Death of Dvorák; London Symphony Orchestra founded; first transmission of music at Graz, Austria

1905 Claude Debussy completes his symphonic suite *La Mer*

1907 Death of Grieg

1910 Birth of Barber

1913 Birth of Britten; Igor Stravinsky composes *Rite of Spring*

1914 Start of World War I

1916 Death of Mahler

1917 Russian Revolution leads to emigration of composers such as Rachmaninov

1918 Death of Debussy

1920 First commercial radio broadcasts made in Pittsburgh, USA; November 11 sees the London Symphony Orchestra conducted by Albert Coates perform the first public rendition of Holst's *The Planets*

1922 Gershwin writes *Rhapsody in Blue*

1928 Ravel's *Boléro* premiers at the Paris Opéra

1924 Death of Fauré; death of Puccini

1934 Death of Delius; death of Elgar; death of Holst

1936 Death of Respighi

1943 Béla Bartók finishes his *Concerto for Orchestra* which premiers on December 1, 1944 in the Boston Symphony Hall played by the Boston Symphony Orchestra conducted by Serge Koussevitzky

1944 Premier of Aaron Copeland's *Appalachian Spring Suite* at the Library of Congress in Washington, D.C.

1948 The LP record introduced by Columbia

1949 Death of Strauss (Richard)

1957 Death of Sibelius

1958 Death of Vaughan Williams

1976 Death of Britten

1981 Death of Barber; first CD pressed in Germany is a recording of Richard Strauss's *Eine Alpensinfonie (An Alpine Symphony)* played by the Berlin Philharmonic Orchestra, conducted by Herbert von Karajan

1 EARLY AND RENAISSANCE MUSIC

"And I spoke and wrote these things not by the invention of my heart or that of any other person, but as by the secret mysteries of God I heard and received them in the heavenly places. And again I heard a voice from Heaven saying to me, "Cry out therefore, and write thus'!" Hildegard von Bingen, Scivias

Early and Renaissance describes the music written prior to the 17th century. As such, it encompasses more than 1000 years of musical tradition, much of it originally founded in the liturgical needs of the Catholic Church, from the decline of the Roman Empire through to the great revolution in the arts that the Renaissance represented. Much of this music was "lost" in subsequent eras and has been rediscovered over the past century as scholarship and interest in musical history have combined. Today, via recordings and downloads, more people are probably listening to medieval music than when it was written.

Classical music has its origins in ancient Greece, where, for example, Pythagoras—better known for this mathematical theorem regarding right-angled triangles—helped to codify musical notation. Early musical instruments, such as the stringed lyre, were also the progenitors of those that would be familiar today to members of the modern orchestra.

The early or medieval period of music runs, effectively from the fall of Rome in the 5th century AD through to the start of the 15th. Much of the music that survives from that period is religious, inevitable given the

Left: Notre Dame, Paris

Above: Religious ceremony: King Louis XII at prayer

Above: Early instruments: Fifteenth–century woodcut depicting Joshua's trumpeters making the walls of Jericho tumble

central role of the church in the life of all and the dominance in education of the monks, nuns and clerics of the period. The most common form of sacred music was plainchant, which was sung in every type of ecclesiastical building.

The most widely practiced form of plainchant is Gregorian, named after Pope Gregory, who was pontiff between 590 and 604 and who was credited with having ordered the simplification and cataloguing of church music. There were, however, other forms of plainchant practiced within the Church. Plainchant was a form of monophonic music that could be sung by an individual or choir. Although a predominantly religious form of music, from the 12th century onwards secular plainchant

music popular with traveling minstrels or troubadours, both male and female. Much of this secular plainchant music was to deal with courtly love and chivalric activities.

Also from the 12th century, monophonic church music was gradually replaced by polyphonic (literally "many-voiced") music which consists of two or more independent melodic voices. It was in the late 12th century that two musicians based at Notre-Dame in Paris–Léonin and Pérotin–are believed to have compiled the first manuscript polyphonic music in Léonin's *Magnus Liber (Great Book)* which was edited by Pérotin.

Left: Gregorian chant: An initial "E" from the Pius II Book of Psalms annotated in Gregorian chant

"Josquin is a master of the notes; they have to do as he wills, while other composers must do as the notes will."

Martin Luther of Josquin des Prés, the first composer of modern music.

The fact that Léonin was able to write down music in manuscript form was a reflection of another of the significant changes of the period: the physical notation of music and the development of the musical score. Prior to this, plainchant had to be learned by the singers and transmitted verbally; inevitably, over time this led to subtle changes. With a score, however, music could be passed in an unchanged form and, with the invention of printing in the mid-15th century, could be disseminated more widely. It was in 1501 that Petrucci invented a means of printing musical scores.

If the period of early music was dominated by the Church, that of the Renaissance was marked by the increased wealth of the aristocracy and the merchants. This increased wealth encouraged many to become involved in the arts, of which music was central, through patronage. The Renaissance (literally "rebirth") was an era in which arts and sciences underwent radical change, as knowledge and questioning of the established order increased. The great Italian patrons—such as the Medici family in Florence—were prominent in their support of the arts, and it was from this era that instrumental music grew in importance as a means, primarily, of entertaining these patrons.

The Renaissance was, however, also to witness the Reformation and the rise of religious strife within Europe. The scene was set for the next great phase of musical development: the Baroque.

Above: Music as entertainment: King Otto IV of Brandenburg playing chess accompanied by musicians

"Dr Tye was a peevish and humoursome man, especially in his latter dayes, and sometimes playing on ye Organ in ye chap. of qu. Elizab. wh. contained much musick, but little of delight to the ear, she would send ye verger to tell him yt he play'd out of Tune: whereupon he sent word yt her ears were out of Tune." Anthony Wood [1632–1695] on the English composer Christopher Tye

Left: Henry VIII with Prince Edward and Jane Seymour in a painting at Hampton Court Palace

TALLIS

Entered here doth ly a worthy wyght,
Who for long tyme in musick bore the bell:
His name to shew, was THOMAS TALLYS hyght,
In honest virtuous lyff he dyd excell.
He serv'd long tyme in chappel with grete prayse
Fower sovereygnes reygnes (a thing not often seen);
I meane Kyng Henry and Prynce Edward's dayes,
Quene Mary, and Elizabeth oure Quene
Attributed memorial to Thomas Tallis on his grave from St Alfege's
Church in London where Tallis was buried and which was rebuilt in
the early 18th century

The 16th century, during which Thomas Tallis was a towering figure in English liturgical music, was a period of great religious turmoil, and Tallis's music reflected the controversies of the age as he produced compositions for both the Catholic and Protestant establishments.

Born during the first decade of the 16th century, probably around 1505, little is known about Tallis's early life. However, he was brought up a Catholic and remained one throughout his life despite the undoubted pressures that he would have been under, particularly after 1558 and the accession of Elizabeth, to conform to the newly established Church. His first musical positions were within the Church, and in 1531 he was appointed organist at

Dover Priory, a Benedictine house in Kent, where he was to remain until 1537 when he moved to London and started to work at St Mary-at-Hill.

The following year he became organist at the Augustinian abbey of Holy Cross at Waltham Abbey; however, Henry VIII had by now broken with Rome and the campaign to dissolve the monasteries had already started. Waltham Abbey was to be the last abbey to be

dissolved when it finally succumbed to the King's Commissioners in 1540.

Tallis then moved to Canterbury Cathedral, were he was to remain for three years until, in 1543, he was sent to the court and became a Gentleman of the Chapel Royal. For the next 42 years, until his death in 1585, Tallis was to serve as organist and composer within the Chapel Royal.

Married in 1552, he was granted a manor in Kent by Queen Mary that provided him with a regular income. This was supplemented in 1575 when Elizabeth awarded him and William Byrd a 21-year monopoly for the right to print and publish sheet music. Amongst the works that they published was *Cantiones sacrae*, the first collection of hymns and motets to be published in England. Tallis was to die on November 23, 1585, at his house in Greenwich and he was buried in St Alfege's Church in Greenwich, although the church collapsed in 1710 following a storm and was subsequently rebuilt to a design by Nicholas Hawksmoor. During the reconstruction, Tallis's tomb was destroyed.

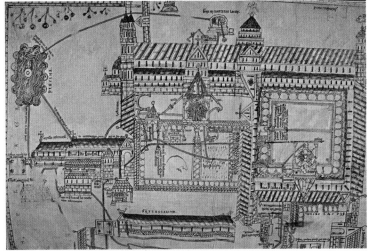

Above: A twelfth-century plan of Canterbury Cathedral, where Tallis played the organ

Left: Dover Castle is close to where Tallis lived and worked

The early compositions produced by Tallis were antiphonal devotions, such as *Salve intemerata virgo*—typical of English liturgical music prior to Henry's break with Rome. It was, however, during the short-lived reign of Edward VI that revised Anglican liturgy first made its appearance, and Tallis was one of the first composers to write anthems in English. The death of Edward and the accession of Mary in 1553, however, brought the Catholic tradition back into fashion and Tallis composed numerous pieces during this period, including *Puer natus est nobis* (Christmas Mass; 1554), one of the few pieces of music that can be accurately dated.

The Catholic revival sparked by Mary's accession was also to be short-lived as, in 1558, Elizabeth came to throne. Under the new monarch the religious mood hardened and became more overtly Protestant. Tallis continued to compose for the rest of his life, although he was notably more conservative than some of his younger contemporaries such as William Byrd.

TALLIS

BORN: c1505, birthplace uncertain

DIED: 1585 in Greenwich, England

INFLUENCED: Vaughan Williams

KEY PIECES

O Nata Lux de Lumine

If You Love Me

Lamentations of Jeremiah

Laudate Dominum

Puer natus est nobis (Christmas Mass; 1554)

Spem in Alium, Nunquam Habui (c1573)

Left: St Alfege's Church, Greenwich, where Tallis was buried before his tomb was destroyed in the 18th century

OTHER EARLY AND RENAISSANCE COMPOSERS

• **Guillaume Dufay** *(1397–1474)* Belgian by birth, Dufay composed widely for both secular and religious purposes; his notable works include *Missa "L'Homme Armé" (Mass of the Armed Man)*, which he completed in the 1450s.

• **John Dunstable** *(1390–1453)* Hugely influential at the time, so much so that some of the radical changes in music of this period are erroneously ascribed to him (such as the development of counterpoint). Dunstable was an English composer whose work was to have an impact across Europe. He wrote much ecclesiastical music, although some of the pieces attributed to him are possibly by his contemporaries.

• **Hildegard of Bingen** *(1098–1179)* A German nun who became abbess of the newly–founded nunnery at Bingen in c1147, Hildegard was an influential poet, diplomat and composer–all very unusual for a woman at this date. Her music is largely formed of single-line setting of religious text.

• **Guillaume de Machaut** *(c1300–1377)* Although a priest, the French-born de Machaut composed both secular and religious music. In his piece *De Touts Flours* he was one of the first composers to use polyphonic settings of poetry. This structure was to be important until the late 15th century. Another notable piece was his *Messe de Notre Dame (Mass of Our Lady)*, his only setting of the mass, which was completed in c1363.

Above: Hildegard of Bingen's manuscript illumination of Universal Man

• **Johannes Ockeghem** *(c1414–1497)* Again hailing from the Low Countries, Ockeghem was a court musician for the French King Charles VII. He also acted as a diplomat for the French. He composed both secular and religious music; like Dufay, his notable works include a setting of the *Missa "L'Homme Armé"* also completed in the 1450s.

• **Giovanni Pierluigi da Palestrina** *(c1525–1594)* The Italian composer Palestrina was one of the most prolific of the late Renaissance composers and the one whose works form the apogee of the contrapuntal style. Some 650 compositions, the vast bulk of them religious, have been attributed to Palestrina; these include the *Missa Brevis (Short Mass)* of 1570 and *The Lamentations of Jeremiah* that date to 1588.

• **John Taverner** *(1490–1545)* Not to be confused with the modern John Tavener (born 1944), this English composer was a believer in the Protestant Reformation and worked alongside Thomas Cromwell. He was also an organist, teacher and singer, and his musical output was largely religious, including his *Magnificat* of c1540.

Right: Giovanni Palestrina, sixteenth-century Italian composer

2 BAROQUE MUSIC

"The end of all good music is to affect the soul."
Claudio Monteverdi

Extending for some 150 years from the early 17th century through to the mid-18th, the Baroque era in classical music was a pivotal time in the development of music, witnessing the growth of the orchestra, the birth of opera and the development of many of the musical terms and concepts that still persist. The word "baroque", derived from the Portuguese word *barroco* ("misshapen pearl"), was originally a pejorative comment upon the heavy architectural style of the period, but by the time it was adopted by scholars to refer to this period of musical evolution, it had lost much of this negativity. It was only in the 20th century that the term became widely used to define the music that was composed between the Renaissance and Classical eras.

It was not only in music that the period witnessed huge creativity—in literature through figures such as Shakespeare and Cervantes; art, with artists like Rembrandt and Rubens; architecture, with architects such as Sir Christopher Wren, Nicholas Hawksmoor and Sir John Vanburgh; and science, with knowledge increased through noted scientists like Galileo and Sir Isaac Newton—the era saw a golden age of the arts and of increased human knowledge.

Baroque music, like the music of the Renaissance, made much use of polyphony and counterpoint, but it

Right: Engraving of a traditional eighteenth-century chamber orchestra

differed from the earlier period in its application of these techniques. In place of complex interwoven parts, Baroque music placed a solo voice or instrument above a single accompaniment consisting of a bass line. The new technique, which arose from the 1590s, was named *secondo prattica* ("second practice") by Claudio Monteverdi to differentiate it from the *primo prattica* ("first practice") of the Renaissance era. The bass line had its chords lightly filled in above; this became known as the *basso continuo* ("continuous bass") and the combination of the *basso continuo* with solo voice became known as "monody" (derived from the Greek for "one song").

There are other differences between

"Perfect and rare virtuoso."

Johann Pachelbel, referred to by his patron, the Duke of Saxe–Eisensach

Left: Baroque architecture: a geometrical elevation of the west end of St. Paul's Cathedral

Baroque and Renaissance music. The former was more often written for virtuoso singers and instrumentalists and was often harder to perform. Baroque music tended towards more ornamentation, often improvised by the performer, with instruments playing a greater role. The tradition of *a cappella* ("in the manner of the church") singing–where a group sings the music without accompaniment by any instrument–became less significant.

One of the consequences of the development of the monody was the birth of opera. This method of singing allowed the composer to ensure that the audience could hear the text clearly through the medium of a single voice, whilst soloists were able much more to interpret the music in a dramatic way. It is generally recognized that the invention of opera was the work of the Camerata–a group that included Florentine musicians active at the end of the 16th century.

This group, which met at the court of Count Giovanni De'Bardi, included the composers Giulio Caccini and Jacopo Peri, as well as the poet Ottavio Rinuccini. As a group they were interested in the classics and in particular ancient Greek musical drama. The work of this trio resulted in the completion in 1598 of *Dafne*, widely regarded as the first true opera. This was followed in 1600 by *Euridice*.

Claudio Monteverdi–who believed that there was a secular application to the combination of harmony and text, and who was to become the most visible of the composers of this generation–composed *Orfeo* in 1607. *Orfeo* became a benchmark for the demonstration of the effects and techniques associated with this new school of music.

Opera required a stage suitable for its performance, and the Baroque period saw the construction of the first specialized auditoria for this purpose. The first public opera house opened in Venice in 1638 and similar facilities were soon to follow in major cities throughout Europe. The cost of staging opera, however, with its hugely expensive sets and special effects, meant that ticket prices were high (some things never change!), and thus it was

"More perfectly executed than anything before them." Johann Gottfried Walther on the vocal pieces composed by Johann Pachelbel

perceived very much as an entertainment for the elite.

Not all appreciated the non–sacred nature of opera; the Catholic church, in particular, was antipathetic and often banned operas during religious festivals such as Lent. Thus, alongside opera there grew up a sacred version of Baroque music–the oratorio. By the end of the Baroque period the oratorio was to reach its apogee in works like Handel's *The Messiah* and Haydn's magnificent *The Creation*.

Apart from the development of opera, the Baroque period also saw the birth of the orchestra and the rise in the importance of instruments. Many of the noted composers and musicians of the period were employed by the courts of the royal families and the aristocracy of Europe, courts that maintained small ensembles of musicians to play the new compositions for entertainment. Chamber music flourished during this era and instruments such as the violin, with its considerable range, came to prominence. For productions of operas, however, the small ensembles were inadequate and the orchestra was born.

By the middle of the 18th century, however, there was an increasing reaction against the complexity and ornamentation of Baroque music, and this led to the rise of the next phase–Classicism.

CORELLI

"The name of Archangelo Corelli will always be of prime importance in the history of the concerto grosso" From The Pelican History of Music 2: Renaissance and Baroque, *edited by Alec Robertson and Denis Stevens*

Born in Fusignano, near Bologna, on February 17, 1653, Arcangelo Corelli—known as *Il Divino* (The Divine)—was a noted violinist as well as a composer who, despite his Italian roots, first came to prominence in Paris in 1672. Although we know relatively little about his early years, it *is* known that he was trained on the violin by Giovanni Battista Bassani and in composition by Matteo Simonelli.

From France he was next to work in Germany where, from 1681 he was employed by the Elector of Bavaria. He returned to Italy a few years later and was based in Rome from 1685 to 1689 where he received patronage from the exiled Queen Christina of Sweden and of Cardinal Pietro Ottoboni (nephew of the future Pope Alexander VIII who was elected to the Holy See in 1689). He lived in Modena from 1689 to 1690 where he received the patronage of the Duke of Modena. He spent the rest of his life in Italy, traveling in 1708 to Rome and Naples.

Apart from his own compositional work, Corelli was also a conductor of operas, oratorios and other large–scale works. Amongst composers whose works he conducted in Italy were pieces by Handel, whose oratorio *Il Trionfo del Tempo e Disinganno (The Triumph of Time and Truth)* was to receive its première in Rome during 1708.

The style of execution introduced by Corelli and preserved by his pupils was of vital importance for the development of violin playing. It has been said that the paths of all of the famous violinist–composers of eighteenth–century Italy led to Arcangelo Corelli. However, Corelli used only a limited portion of his instrument's capabilities.

This may be seen from his writings: the parts for violin very rarely proceed above D on the highest string, sometimes reaching the E in fourth position on the highest string. It has been claimed that Corelli refused to play a passage that extended to A in altissimo in the overture to Handel's *Il Trionfo del Tempo e Disinganno* and took serious offense when the composer (32 years his junior) played the note. Nevertheless, his compositions for the instrument mark an epoch in the history of chamber music. His influence was not confined to his own country. Johann Sebastian Bach studied Corelli's works and based an organ fugue (BWV 579) on Corelli's Opus 3 of 1689.

Musical society in Rome also owed much to Corelli. He was received in the highest circles of the aristocracy,

CORELLI: VIOLIN VIRTUOSO OF THE "DOUBLE-STOP" TECHNIQUE

As a violin virtuoso, Corelli is credited with helping to pioneer the technique of "double stopping"—the act of playing two notes simultaneously—and he was central to the development of modern techniques of using the bow. In performing a double stop, two separate strings are depressed ("stopped") by the fingers, and bowed or plucked simultaneously without a string change.

According to Cecil Forsyth's book Orchestration [Macmillan 1914, reprinted by Dover in 1982] the invention of the double-stop is generally credited to Carlo Farina, an Italian composer, conductor and violinist of the Baroque era, whose Capriccio Stravagante (1627) was published in Dresden while he was Court-Violinist at Saxony.

The website The Violin Site (www.theviolinsite.com), warns beginners that double stopping is much harder than normal single-string playing, as more than one finger has to be accurately placed on two different strings simultaneously. "Sometimes, moving to a higher position is necessary in order for it to be physically possible for the fingers to be placed in the correct places. Double stopping is also used to mean playing on three or all four strings at once, although such practices are more properly called triple or

Above: Corelli was central to the development of modern violin techniques of using the bow

quadruple stopping. Collectively, double, triple and quadruple stopping is called multiple stopping."

The violinist and author Clayton Haslop [violinmastery.com] tempers that double-stop playing requires patience and discipline, "perhaps even a willingness to endure a little discomfort, for the mildly arthritic", but he adds that the rewards for staying the course are "wonderful, and almost unique in the world of music".

"The challenge is to really get the control of your hands and ear necessary to do them beautifully and easily," says Haslop. "It has been such a challenge, in fact, that many a pedagogue and performer have written volumes of etudes on the subject. Now here's a little tip or two on the subject. Number one, don't over press with your fingers; play with the minimum of pressure possible. I don't even push the strings down to the fingerboard unless I'm required to play fortissimo."

Above: Queen Christina of Sweden

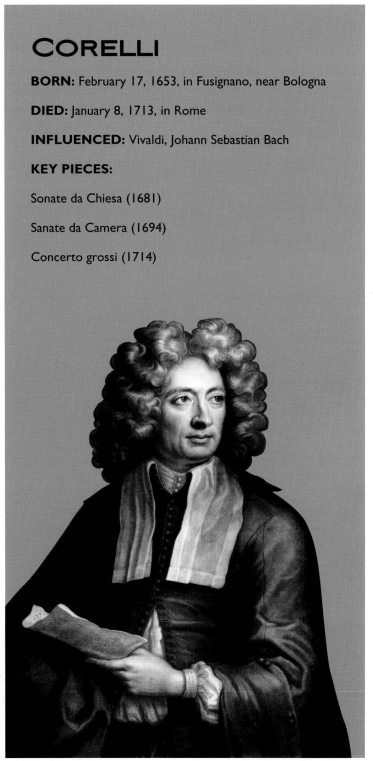

CORELLI

BORN: February 17, 1653, in Fusignano, near Bologna

DIED: January 8, 1713, in Rome

INFLUENCED: Vivaldi, Johann Sebastian Bach

KEY PIECES:

Sonate da Chiesa (1681)

Sanate da Camera (1694)

Concerto grossi (1714)

and for a long time presided at the celebrated Monday concerts in the palace of Cardinal Ottoboni. As a violin virtuoso, he was central to the development of modern techniques of using the bow, and was one of the earliest to use the effect of double stopping on the instrument. His compositions are distinguished by a beautiful flow of melody and by a mannerly treatment of the accompanying parts, which he is justly said to have liberated from the strict rules of counterpoint.

Corelli died on January 8,1713, leaving a considerable fortune and an impressive collection of art works. He was buried in the Pantheon in Rome.

PURCELL

"Music is the exultation of poetry. Both of them may excel apart but surely they are most excellent when they are joined, because nothing is then wanting to either of their proportions; for thus they appear like wit and beauty in the same person."
Preface to Dioclesian,*1690*

The son of a court musician and chorister of the Chapel Royal who had sung at the Coronation of King Charles II, Henry Purcell's actual birth date is open to some debate, although it is widely believed to have been September 11,1659. Born in London, Purcell was to pass to the guardianship of an uncle in 1664 following the death of his father, and through his uncle, who was also a chorister of the Chapel Royal, Purcell was admitted as a child chorister.

He studied music initially under Henry Cooke and later Pelham Humphrey, singing in the choir until his voice broke in 1673. He was then appointed assistant to John Hingeston, the keeper of musical instruments for the king, although he continued his studies under John Blow following the death of Humphrey in 1674, and was also a student at Westminster School. In 1677 he succeeded Matthew Locke as composer for the king's violins. He was subsequently appointed organist of Westminster Abbey in 1679, following the resignation of John Blow, and

Right: The Chapel Royal in Hampton Court Palace

organist of the Chapel Royal, in succession to Edward Lowe, three years later.

Purcell is believed to have been composing from an early age, although the first piece of music that can be directly attributed to him is an ode composed for King Charles's birthday in 1670. During the 1670s he composed both for the church and for the theater; his works later in the decade for the latter included the music for *Theodosius* and *Virtuous Wife*. Following his appointment as organist at Westminster Abbey, however, Purcell's compositions were almost exclusively sacred, as he largely foreswore his earlier interest in the theater.

LES CLAVECINISTES

Purcell married in 1682, fathering six children, four of whom died in infancy. Later the same year he was appointed organist of the Chapel Royal, whilst continuing to be the organist at Westminster Abbey. As such, he was involved in the composing of music for many of the great state occasions, such as the coronation of King James II in 1685, for which he composed two of his best-known anthems, *I Was Glad* and *My Heart Is Inditing*. He was also responsible for co–coordinating the music and composing additional pieces for the funeral of Queen Mary after her death in December 1694.

In the late 1680s he returned once again to the production of large–scale secular music. In 1689 he completed the score for the opera *Dido and Aeneas*, which is considered to be one of the first operas to be completed by an Englishman. For the rest of his life he continued to compose both for the church and for the theater, completing the scores for no fewer than 42 plays between 1689 and 1695.

Henry Purcell died on November 21,1695, at his home in Dean's Yard, Westminster. Following his funeral, at which the music that he'd arranged for the funeral of Queen Mary was played, he was buried near the organ in the abbey.

"Here lyes Henry Purcell Esq., who left this life and is gone to that blessed place where only his harmony can be exceeded."
Epitaph in Westminster Abbey

Top left: An engraving of the seventeenth-century waterfront at Westminster, London, at the time when Purcell was organist at Westminster Abbey

Bottom left: Sarah Connolly as Dido in the Royal Opera's production of Purcell's Dido and Aeneas

PURCELL

BORN: Circa September 11, 1659, in London

DIED: November 21,1695, in London

INFLUENCED BY: Blow, Locke and continental practice

INFLUENCED: Britten

KEY PIECES

Ode for St Cecilia's Day (1683)

Dido and Aeneas (1689)

King Arthur (1691)

The Fairy Queen (1692)

The Indian Queen (1695)

VIVALDI

"I have heard him boast of composing a concerto faster than a copyist could write it down!" Charles de Brosse,1739

Born in Venice on March 4,1678, and nicknamed *il Prete Rosso* (the Red Priest) after the color of his hair, Antonio Lucio Vivaldi is today best known as the composer of *The Four Seasons*, a series of four violin concertos composed in 1723 whilst Vivaldi was living in Rome and published two year later. He was, however, also a highly accomplished violinist, playing in the city whilst he trained to become a priest.

His father, Giovanni, a barber who subsequently became a professional violinist, tutored his son in music. Giovanni was also one of the founders of the *Sovvegno dei Musicisti di Santa Cecilia*, an association of musicians whose president was Giovanni Legrenzi, at that time music master at St Mark's in Venice, and it is possible that the young Vivaldi was taught composition by Legrenzi.

In September 1703 Vivaldi was appointed master of violins at the *Conservatorio dell'Ospedale della Pietà* (Devout Hospital of Mercy) in Venice. This was one of a number of orphanages in the city that offered boys training in a trade and girls an education in music. It also offered accommodation to abandoned but

talented girls, and under Vivaldi's guidance the reputation of the institution for its music grew immensely.

Vivaldi was associated with the hospital for some 30 years—although not continuously, as his position was subject to annual review, and in 1709 he was voted out of office and spent a year away. He composed some of his

Right: An early map of Venice

Above: Vivaldi with violin

Armonico (Harmonic Inspiration)-that was first published in 1711. The music was dedicated to Grand Prince Ferdinand of Tuscany, a noted sponsor of composers at the time who also supported Handel.

Much of the music composed for the hospital was sacred but Vivaldi was also to find fame as a composer of music for the Venice opera, which was the most important form of popular entertainment in the city at that time. Apart from actually composing opera–such as *Ottone in Villa*, first performed in Vicenza in 1713–Vivaldi was also an impresario, taking control of the Teatro Sant'Angelo in 1714. Alongside this commercial work, Vivaldi continued to compose sacred music, most notably *Juditha Triumphans (Judith Victorious)* in 1716. This was written to mark the victory of Venice over the Turks and the recapture of the island of Corfu.

In either 1717 or 1718 Vivaldi was appointed the *Maestro di Cappella* for the governor of Mantua, Prince Phillip of Hesse-Darmstadt, and during his three years in Mantua he composed several operas. He visited Milan in 1721 and 1722, before reaching Rome later in 1722. During this period he composed the piece for which he is now best remembered: *Le quattro stagioni (The Four Seasons)* first published in 1725, the year that Vivaldi returned to Venice.

However, during his period in Milan, Vivaldi had met the young singer Anna Tessieri Giro, who was to become

most important works whilst based there and became musical director of the hospital in 1716. It was during the first decade of the 18th century that Vivaldi started to compose but his reputation around Europe was first established with the 12 concerti for violins–*L'Estro*

his student. Although there is no evidence of any physical relationship between priest and pupil, rumors about their friendship were to plague his later life.

As Vivaldi's fame spread, he traveled further afield, reaching Vienna and Prague in 1730, where his opera *Farnace (Pharnaces)* was to receive its première. He was to become music director at the court of the Emperor, Charles VI, in 1740, but his later life, which he spent largely in Vienna, was dogged by his increasing ill–health—he probably had suffered from asthma for much of his life—and by financial problems, particularly after the death of his patron Charles VI, as the popularity of the Venice opera declined. Vivaldi himself was to die shortly after Charles, during the night of July 27/28, 1741, in a house owned by the widow of a Viennese saddle-maker. He was buried in the churchyard of St George's Church in Vienna after a funeral in St Stephen's Cathedral, at which the young Joseph Haydn was a chorister.

"Vivaldi played a solo accompaniment excellently, and at the conclusion he added a free fantasy which absolutely astounded me, for it is hardly possible that anyone has ever played, or ever will play, in such a fashion."
Johann Armand von Uffenbach

VIVALDI

BORN: March 4, 1678, in Venice

DIED: July 27/28, 1741, in Vienna

INFLUENCED: Bach

KEY PIECES

L'Estro Armonico (Harmonic Inspiration) (1711)

Juditha Triumphans (Judith Victorious) (1716)

Le quattro stagioni (The Four Seasons) (1725)

HANDEL

"The master of us all... the greatest composer that ever lived. I would uncover my head and kneel before his tomb."
Beethoven

Although born in Germany, on February 23, 1685, as Georg Friedrich Händel, George Frederic Handel, as his name became anglicized, was perhaps the most significant composer to be based in Britain during the 18th century. He lived predominantly in Britain from 1710 and was to compose much of his most famous music in the country and in English. He became a British citizen in 1727 and died in London in 1759. He was buried in Westminster Abbey.

Handel was born in Halle, then part of the Duchy of Magdeburg, where his father was barber–surgeon. Initially the family was antipathetic towards Handel's interest in music but, once convinced of the boy's talents, his father permitted him to study music under Friedrich Wilhelm Zachow, the organist of Halle's Marienkirche. His reputation grew quickly and in 1698 he played in front of King Frederick I in Berlin. In 1702, following his father's wishes, he started to study law at the University of Halle whilst at the same time he obtained a position as organist at the city's cathedral, but this

arrangement lasted for only a year as, in 1703, he moved to Hamburg where he joined the orchestra of the opera house.

It was at Hamburg, in 1705, that he composed his first major works—the operas *Almira* and *Nero*. The following year, after an invitation from a member of the de Medici family, he went to Florence and then to Rome. With opera being banned in the latter city at the time, he turned his attention to sacred music, composing *Dixit Dominus* during this period. However, he went on

Left: The young Handel playing the cembalo

Above: Plaque on Fishamble Street, Dublin, commemorating the first performance of Handel's Messiah *in Mr Neales Music Hall in 1742*

Left: Handel's oratorio Solomon *was first performed at the Covent Garden Theatre, London, on 17 March 1749*

to compose more operas, achieving considerable success in both Florence and Venice.

In 1710 he became Kapellmeister (Director of Music) to George, Elector of Hanover, a position that was to prove pivotal to Handel's career for two reasons. Firstly, the position allowed for considerable travel, enabling Handel to make his first trip to Britain. (It's possible that his employer rather resented Handel's prolonged periods of absence and it is thought that the *Water Music* of 1717 was a peace offering.) Secondly, in 1714 George succeeded to the throne of the United Kingdom, thus giving Handel a position within the British cultural establishment. As a result he wrote a considerable amount of music for state occasions, such as the music composed for the coronation of King George II in 1727 that included the anthem *Zadok the Priest*, which has been performed at every British coronation since.

Apart from his role in the provision of music for state occasions, Handel was also heavily involved in the commercial musical theater, as well as being a canny investor. He was one of the few to make money out of

Above: Handel presenting his Water Music to King George I

Pages 52–53: A facsimile from the Belshazzar oratorio in the Handel House in Halle Saale, Germany

HANDEL

BORN: February 23, 1685, in Halle, Germany

DIED: April 14, 1759, in London

KEY PIECES

Dixit Dominus (1707)

Utrecht te Deum (1713)

Water Music (1717)

Giulio Cesare in Egitto (Julius Caesar in Egypt) (1724)

Zadok the Priest (1727)

Esther (1735)

Messiah (1742)

Music for the Royal Firework (1749)

Jephtha (1752)

the South Sea Bubble, withdrawing his funds before the great collapse. Commercially he was involved with the Royal Academy of Music, the King's theater and with the Covent Garden theater. But by the mid–1730s the fashion for the Italian-style opera that Handel had initially popularized had declined, and this, combined with a marked deterioration in his health in 1737, led to a significant change of direction–the development of the English oratorio. The new style was best exemplified by the première of the *Messiah* in Dublin on April 13, 1742.

He continued to compose during the 1740s, with such notable works as *Music for the Royal Fireworks* appearing during these years. However, he was seriously injured in a carriage accident in August 1750 whilst traveling back to Britain from Germany, and the following year his eyesight started to deteriorate. Despite these problems he continued to compose, producing his final great oratorio, *Jephtha*, in 1752.

Handel died on April 14, 1759. Unmarried, the bulk of his £20,000 fortune–a vast sum for the period–was bequeathed to a niece in Germany.

BACH

"The aim and final end of all music should be none other than the glory of God and the refreshment of the soul."
Bach

Now regarded as one of the key composers of the late Baroque period, to contemporaries Johann Sebastian Bach was better known as an organist, overshadowed by his sons in the art of composing. However, rediscovered towards the end of the 18th century, his work is now regarded as amongst the most important of the first half of that century.

Bach was born on March 31, 1685, in Eisenach, Germany, the son of Johann Ambrosius Bach, the director of the town's musicians, and Maria Elisabeth Lämmerhirt. Following the death of his mother in 1684 and his father–who had initially taught him to play the violin and harpsichord–the following year, the young Bach moved in with his elder brother, Johann Christoph, who was by this stage the organist at St Michael's Church in Orhrdruf. It was his brother who introduced Bach to organ playing. At the age of 14, Bach was awarded a choral scholarship to the highly selective St Michael's School, Lüneberg, where he studied for two years. Apart from music, Bach learnt languages and other academic subjects and was brought into contact with the sons of many of the prominent families of northern Germany.

Following a brief period as a court musician in the chapel of Duke Johann Ernst in Weimar, Bach was appointed organist at St Boniface's Church in Arnstadt in August 1703. His duties allowed Bach to start compositional work, although his period at Arnstadt was not always harmonious. He took unauthorized leave to visit the organist Dietrich Buxtehude at Lübeck, some 250 miles distant, and in August 1705 was almost involved in a duel with a student. Thus, despite the comfort of his position, Bach decided in 1707 to become organist at St Blasius's Church in Mülhausen. It was while living in Mülhausen that Bach married his second cousin, Maria Barbara Bach. They had seven children, two of whom–Wilhelm Friedemann and Carl Philipp–became composers in their own right and whose work, for a period, overshadowed that of their father.

Bach, despite overseeing the construction of a new organ at Mülhausen, spent only a year in the city before, in 1708, becoming the court organist and music master to the court of the Duke of Weimar. Although Bach prospered professionally at Weimar, composing both keyboard and orchestral music, he gradually fell out of favor and was eventually dismissed in 1717 after having spent a month in jail.

From Weimar, Bach moved to Köthen where he

Above: Mulhausen, where Bach lived and worked as organist at the St Blasius Church

Below: Leipzig, where Bach started his musical career

became director of music to Prince Leopold, Prince of Anhalt–Köthen, where he was to stay for six years. Prince Leopold was a Calvanist and therefore during these years the bulk of Bach's compositions were of a secular nature, such as the *Brandenburg Concertos* of 1721.

Bach's first wife died in 1720 while they were living at Köthen, and he remarried in 1721, this time to Anna Magdalena Wilcke, with whom he had a further thirteen children. Three of the sons of this union were also to become prominent musicians.

After six years in Költen, and following the death of Prince Leopold, Bach moved in 1723 to Leipzig where he became Cantor of St Thomas's School. In the years following he produced the majority of his cantatas and, in 1724, his *St John Passion* received its première. Other prominent religious pieces from this period include his *St Matthew Passion*, first performed in 1729. In March that year he became the director of the Collegium Musicum, originally established in 1701, an ensemble that specialized in the playing of secular music.

In 1733 Bach composed the Kyrie and Gloria of what later became his *Mass in B Minor*, which was not completed until the next decade. The manuscript was presented to August III, Elector of Saxony and King of Poland, as part of Bach's ultimately successful attempt to be appointed court composer.

The composer's eyesight began to fail in 1746, although the following year he managed to visit Potsdam to visit his son Carl Philipp Emanuel, who was employed by Frederick the Great. Whilst there he played for the king, and one of the improvised pieces that he performed was later to become *A Musical Offering*. Returning to Leipzig, Bach continued work on his final masterpiece–*The Art of Fuge*–which was destined to be unfinished at his death on July 28, 1750, following an unsuccessful operation to improve his sight by the celebrated British surgeon John Taylor.

"The immortal god of harmony." Beethoven, in a letter to Christoph Breitkopf in 1801

Above: A stained—glass window in Saint Thomas Church, Leipzig, Germany, commemorates the time Johann Sebastian Bach worked there as a choirmaster.

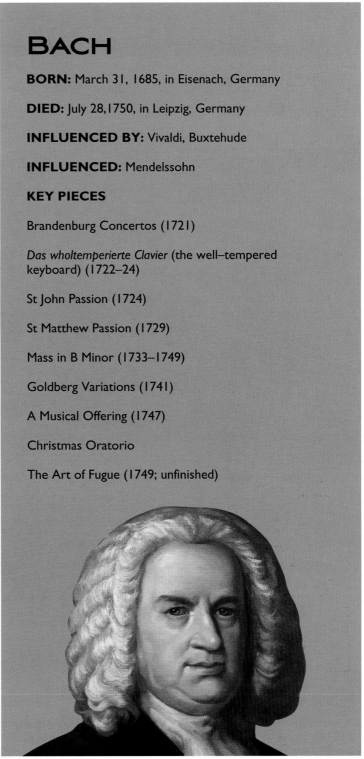

BACH

BORN: March 31, 1685, in Eisenach, Germany

DIED: July 28, 1750, in Leipzig, Germany

INFLUENCED BY: Vivaldi, Buxtehude

INFLUENCED: Mendelssohn

KEY PIECES

Brandenburg Concertos (1721)

Das wholtemperierte Clavier (the well—tempered keyboard) (1722–24)

St John Passion (1724)

St Matthew Passion (1729)

Mass in B Minor (1733–1749)

Goldberg Variations (1741)

A Musical Offering (1747)

Christmas Oratorio

The Art of Fugue (1749; unfinished)

OTHER BAROQUE COMPOSERS

Above: Jean-Philippe Rameau

• **Marc-Antoine Charpentier** *(1643–1794)* French composer of both religious and non–religious settings; notable works include his *Christmas Oratorio*.

• **Francois Couperin** *(1668–1733)* French-born organist from a family of musicians who composed widely for keyboard instruments, most notably the harpsichord.

• **Orlando Gibbons** *(1583–1627)* English organist and composer whose work included madrigals and church music.

• **John-Baptiste Lully** *(1632–1687)* Born in Italy but brought up in France, Lully was court musician to Louis XIV (The Sun King) and exercised almost total control over French music for some twenty–five years.

• **Claudio Monteverdi** *(1567–1643)* Italian composer whose music includes both sacred and secular. Was a pioneer in the development of opera.

• **Johann Pachelbel** *(1653–1706)* German organist and composer who was one of the major keyboard musicians of the 18th century. Perhaps best–known today for his *Canon in D* (as featured on the accompanying disc to this book).

• **Jean-Philippe Rameau** *(1683–1764)* The most important French composer of the 18th century, Rameau was also a musical theorist whose work was highly influential. He composed a number of pieces for keyboard instruments and his first opera was completed at the age of 50.

• **Domenico Scarlatti** *(1685–1757)* Born into a musical family in Italy, Scarlatti was a keyboard virtuoso and composer.

• **Georg Philipp Telemann** *(1681–1767)* Born in Germany, Telemann was one of the most prolific composers of the later Baroque period. He wrote more than 3,500 pieces, including some fifty operas.

Above: Jean-Baptiste Lully

Right : Domenico Scarletti

3 THE CLASSICAL PERIOD

"My Prince was always satisfied… and I was in a position to improve, alter, and be as bold as I pleased."
Haydn, on his employer Prince Nicolaus Esterházy

Although the word "classical" is used widely to cover the whole canon of largely western music from the post-Roman era through to the modern age, it has a much more specific use to describe the music of the period from the mid-18th century through to the early years of the 19th. Although a relatively short time in chronological terms, the period—which extended from the end of the Baroque period to the start of the Romantic—was to see the emergence of some of the most important composers in history, including Joseph Haydn, Wolfgang Amadeus Mozart, Ludwig van Beethoven and Franz Schubert.

Classical music was a reaction against the increasing complexity of Baroque music. It was a simpler style that reflected the burgeoning intellectualism of the 18th century—the Age of Enlightenment—rejecting the polyphony, counterpoint and ornamented melodies of the earlier age in favor of simple melodies with harmonic progressions. This meant that the playing of chords became much more prevalent, resulting in the tonal structure of the works becoming more audible.

The 18th century was an era of significant advance in artistic and economic terms. The rediscovery of Pompeii

Above: Pompeii

had reawakened interest in the true classical era, whilst the Enlightenment had brought new political thought and an increasing belief in personal freedom. It was no coincidence that the end of the century was to be marked by two pivotal moments in world history that represented the overthrow of the established order: the American Declaration of Independence and the French Revolution. The Industrial Revolution, started in Britain in the mid-18th century, was also of fundamental importance in helping to create a new bourgeois class that lacked the inherited wealth of the aristocracy but who aspired to the standards of learning and

knowledge of the arts that the traditional ruling elite had taken for granted.

However, the 18th century was to witness the decline of the aristocratic patronage of classical musicians, as economic hardship resulted in a relative decline in their wealth, but it was also to see the rise of public concerts and "freelance" musicians. Musicians such as Haydn and Mozart, whilst still employed by their patrons, were permitted to travel widely, bringing their music to a much greater audience and being influenced by musical traditions encountered during their travels. By 1794, for example, Beethoven was able to

Above: Adieu Bastille: 1791 cartoon commemorating the French Revolution

move to Vienna and survive, with the support of a number of influential backers, without the official position that had been essential for musicians earlier in the century. The symphony orchestra, albeit smaller than that in use in the 21st century, was also to have its origins during this period.

As the commercial audience became ever more important, so composers had to tailor increasingly their musical output for these audiences. Instrumental music was, for the first time, seen as preferable to vocal, and the era witnessed significant developments in such music. Most notable were the more formal definition of the sonata and concerto, as well as the creation of the symphony—widely credited to Haydn—which grew out of the Baroque sinfonia and was generally to be found with four movements. Historically, the concerto grosso was a piece of music designed for more than one musician; during the classical period it became much more usual to see a solo concerto, where there was a single soloist. This inevitably brought the skills of such musicians into sharp relief, and was an additional factor in the rise of the freelance musician as one who was capable of carving a career in music without the necessity of an official position.

Right: Title page of Mozart's Six String Quartets dedicated to Joseph Haydn and composed between 1782 and 1785

Below: Mozart playing from the score of his opera Don Giovanni *in 1787*

Of all the classical era composers, Joseph Haydn was arguably the most influential in seeing the transition from the Baroque. There were others, such as Handel and Telemann, who transcended the two eras, but it was Haydn who has become known as father of both the symphony and the string quartet. Benefiting from the patronage of the wealthy Esterházy family, but still able to travel widely across Europe, Haydn was able to bring his skills to composing and, when he first met the young Wolfgang Amadeus Mozart who was many years his younger, the two—master and pupil—were able to spark new ideas off each other.

Above: The Votive church, Vienna, 1890

Above: Christoph von Gluck at the spinet

"The art of music here entombed a rich possess, but even fairer hopes. Franz Schubert lies here."
Epitaph on Schubert's grave in Vienna

Although the classical era was in many respects an age when orchestral as opposed to vocal music developed, it did also see the further growth of opera. Traditionally a musical form dominated by the Italians and by the Italian language, increasingly composers from outside Italy, most notably Mozart, started to come to prominence. Apart from Mozart, the German Christoph von Gluck was perhaps one of the most influential figures in the evolution of classical era opera, having abandoned convention in favor of closer relationship between music and drama.

The classical era, with its emphasis upon learning and freedom, was to come crashing down with the bloodshed of the French Revolution and the years of war that resulted. One composer, Ludwig van Beethoven, bestrode this divide like a colossus and it was he who signaled, with his Symphony No. 7 of 1812, the transition to the next great phase of classical music—the Romantic era.

HAYDN

"There was no one near to confuse me, so I was forced to become original."
Haydn

A composer who straddled the Baroque, Classical and Early Romantic periods, Joseph Haydn was one of the most prolific composers of the 18th and 19th centuries, completing almost 1,200 works during his long life. Widely regarded as the "Father of the Symphony" and "Father of the String Quartet" as a result of his contribution to the development of these types of music, Haydn was also to be a major influence on Mozart and Beethoven, two of the principal composers of the next generation.

Born on March 3, 1732, in Austria, Haydn was the son of a wheelwright and a former cook. Although neither parent could read music, Haydn's father was an enthusiastic folk musician and the young Haydn grew up in a family where music was common. It was evident from an early age that the boy had talent, with the result that, at the age of seven, he was sent to study with a relative, Johann Matthias Frankh, who was schoolmaster and choirmaster at nearby Hainburg.

Although Haydn's experiences with Frankh were not always positive, he did learn to play the violin and harpsichord, as well as singing as a treble in the choir. He soon came to the attention of Georg von Reutter, director of

music at St Stephen's Cathedral in Vienna, and following an audition Haydn moved to Vienna in 1740, where he was to remain for nine years and further his musical education. Although Reutter was not to provide Haydn with much tuition in composition, the student was in a musical milieu where he would have learnt a considerable amount simply by being there.

When his voice broke in 1749 Haydn's career in the choir at St Stephen's came to an end. Dismissed for playing a prank, Haydn found himself destitute and cast into the street. For the next few years he struggled to survive, working as a

Left: Engraving of Franz Joseph Haydn conducting a String Quartet

music teacher, a street singer and a valet-accompanist to the Italian composer Nicolo Porpora, who was to aid him in the development of his compositional skills.

Despite the struggle to survive, Haydn continued his musical education–he was later to regard himself as effectively self-taught, through reading treatises and exercises. His major break came, however, in 1753 with the music for the opera *Der krumme Teufel*, which, although subsequently banned, helped further to establish his growing reputation. Although for the next few years Haydn continued to work as a freelance, he was increasingly connected to the establishment and, in 1757, became Kapellmeister (director of music) for Count Morzin. It was whilst with Count Morzin that Haydn composed his first symphonies and also got married. However, his marriage to Maria Anna Aloysia Apollonia Keller in 1760 was a disaster, although no divorce was possible.

In 1761 a decline in Count Morzin's fortunes forced him to dispense with the services of his musicians, and Haydn became vice-kapellmeister to the Esterházy family, then one of the most prominent families in the Austrian Empire. Following the death of Gregor Werner five years later Haydn was promoted to the position of Kapellmeister. Haydn was to remain with the Esterházy family–under princes

Left: Letter from Wolfgang Amadeus Mozart to Franz Joseph Haydn in which Mozart dedicates his six sonatas for pianoforte to Haydn

Below: A bust of the composer Franz Joseph Haydn from the collection of the Musee de l'Homme in Paris.

Paul Anton and Nikolaus I–for the next 25 years, until the death of Nikolaus I in 1790. Although he was to compose a vast amount of music specifically for the family, his fame ensured that he also received commissions from elsewhere, many of which were amongst his most significant works.

Nikolaus I was succeeded by a prince who lacked his predecessor's interest in music and who dismissed the court musicians, placing Haydn on a pension. As a result, Haydn was free to accept an invitation to visit London from the impresario Johann Petyer Salomon. Haydn was ultimately to make two prolonged visits to England–in 1790/91 and 1794/95–during which he composed some of his best-known pieces, including the *Surprise* and *London* symphonies.

In 1795 he was recalled to court by Prince Nikolaus II, who had inherited the title the previous year, and returned to Vienna. The period from 1795 to 1803 witnessed the final flowering of Haydn's output. These included

"My children, have no fear, for where Haydn is, no harm can fall."
Haydn, on his deathbed in 1809, to reassure his servants as Vienna was being attacked by the French

the two great oratorios—*The Creation* and *The Seasons*—plus the Trumpet Concerto and the last nine of his string quartets. However, in 1802, an illness, which had been troubling for some years, grew in severity, making it physically impossible for him to compose, although he was able to continue to play the piano as a relaxation. Haydn died on May 31, 1809, at a time when Vienna was under attack by Napoleon's French army. Mozart's *Requiem* was played at his funeral.

Haydn's music was comprehensively catalogued by Anthony van Hoboken in the 20th century. The catalogue was published in 1957 and Haydn's works are now generally referred to by their Hoboken (either "Hob" or "H") number.

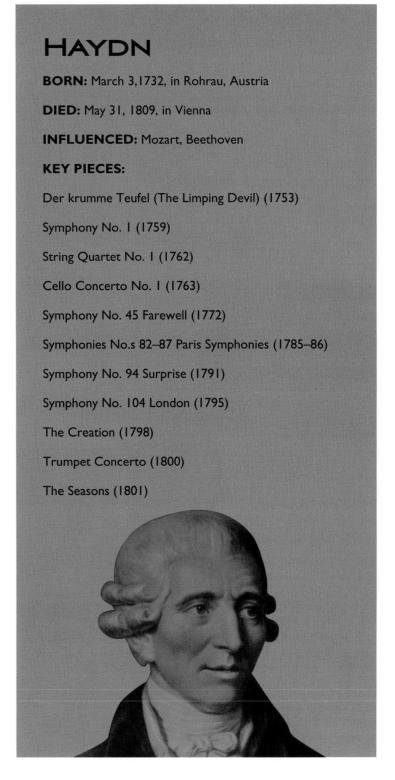

HAYDN

BORN: March 3, 1732, in Rohrau, Austria

DIED: May 31, 1809, in Vienna

INFLUENCED: Mozart, Beethoven

KEY PIECES:

Der krumme Teufel (The Limping Devil) (1753)

Symphony No. 1 (1759)

String Quartet No. 1 (1762)

Cello Concerto No. 1 (1763)

Symphony No. 45 Farewell (1772)

Symphonies No.s 82–87 Paris Symphonies (1785–86)

Symphony No. 94 Surprise (1791)

Symphony No. 104 London (1795)

The Creation (1798)

Trumpet Concerto (1800)

The Seasons (1801)

MOZART

"At the age of five he was already composing little pieces, which he played to his father who wrote them down."
Marie Anna Mozart

Arguably the greatest prodigy in musical history, Johannes Chrysostomus Wolfgangus Theophilus Mozart—better known as Wolfgang Amadeus Mozart—was born in Salzburg, Austria, on January 27, 1756. His father, Leopold, was the deputy Kapellmeister to the court orchestra of the Archbishop of Salzburg, who was also a gifted musician, composer and teacher of music.

From an early age, the young Mozart demonstrated an interest in music, starting to play the clavier from the age of three, learning from his seven-year-old sister Anne Marie (known as Nannerl), who was equally a child prodigy. Leopold was to teach both children a broad range of subjects, not just music, and soon gave up his own musical career in order to promote the talents of his children. From the age of six, Mozart and his family traveled widely around Europe,

Right: Mozart at the age of six playing the organ in the Church of the Franciscans in Vienna

as Leopold demonstrated the precocity of his two children.

The first trip, in 1761, was to Munich, where the Mozarts performed before Maximilian III of Bavaria. Later the same year they visited Vienna and Prague, but the next trip was of more than three years in duration, taking the family to Munich (twice), Mannheim, Paris (twice), London, The Hague, Zürich and Donaueschingen. Whilst in London in 1764 Mozart met Johann Christian Bach, one of Johann Sebastian Bach's sons, for the first time. They were

Above: Wolfgang Amadeus Mozart

and 1773. It was during the second of these trips that he composed the motet *Exsultate, jubilate* for the well-known castrato Venanzio Rauzzini; this remains one of the most popular of his repertoire.

On his return to Salzburg in March 1773 Mozart was appointed a musician to the court of Prince-Archbishop Hieronymus Colloredo, the city's ruler. For the next four years he was to compose a prodigious quantity of music in different genres—symphonies, minor operas and chamber pieces—but found the low salary and an inability to place his operas increasingly problematic. He was able to visit Vienna and Munich during his four years as a court musician but resigned in September 1777 to seek a better paid position.

His next trip, taking in Augsburg, Mannheim, Paris (where his *Paris* Symphony was premièred in 1778) and Munich, was to play a pivotal role in his future life. In Mannheim he met the Weber family, and although initially infatuated with Aloysia, he was eventually to marry her sister Constanze, following his move to Vienna in 1781. The couple were to have six children, of which only two survived to childhood.

Returning to Salzburg in January 1779 he took a new, slightly better paid, position with the court. He was to remain in his home city for a further two years until, following the successful première in Munich of his opera *Idomeneo* in January 1781, he was summoned to the imperial court at Vienna, along with Archbishop Colloredo, who was in the city to help celebrate the accession of Francis II. During the visit Mozart fell out with Colloredo and resigned his position in May 1781. Thereafter, Mozart remained in Vienna, where he composed some 200 pieces, although his break with Colloredo was to lead to an estrangement with Leopold who had supported the archbishop. A visit with his family back to Salzburg in 1783, in an attempt to improve relations with his father and sister, was marked by the composition of the Mass in C Minor.

Initially Mozart's lifestyle in Vienna, funded by the

to meet again in 1765, and between 1767 and 1768 the family was based in Vienna.

In December, leaving his mother and sister in Salzburg, Mozart traveled once more in the company of his father, this time to Italy. This tour was to last until March 1771 and encompassed trips to Bologna, Rome and Milan. Whilst in Milan, in 1770, his opera *Mitridate, re di Ponto* (*Mithridates, King of Pontus*) received its première. Following the family's return to Austria in 1771, Mozart was to visit Milan on two further occasions between then

Above: The Court of Brera, Milan

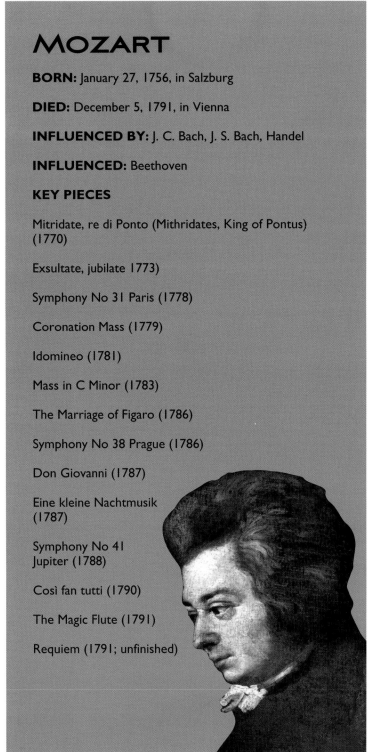

MOZART

BORN: January 27, 1756, in Salzburg

DIED: December 5, 1791, in Vienna

INFLUENCED BY: J. C. Bach, J. S. Bach, Handel

INFLUENCED: Beethoven

KEY PIECES

Mitridate, re di Ponto (Mithridates, King of Pontus) (1770)

Exsultate, jubilate 1773)

Symphony No 31 Paris (1778)

Coronation Mass (1779)

Idomineo (1781)

Mass in C Minor (1783)

The Marriage of Figaro (1786)

Symphony No 38 Prague (1786)

Don Giovanni (1787)

Eine kleine Nachtmusik (1787)

Symphony No 41 Jupiter (1788)

Così fan tutti (1790)

The Magic Flute (1791)

Requiem (1791; unfinished)

success of his musical output, was quite luxurious and the mid-1780s were to witness some of his most important orchestral and operatic pieces, such as *The Marriage of Figaro* and *Don Giovanni*, and he also achieved the position of "chamber composer" to Francis II in 1787. However, in the last years of his life, Mozart's fortunes declined, as Austria was at war with France following the French Revolution of 1789 and there was little aristocratic support for music. He was forced to start borrowing money from friends, give piano lessons and take in lodgers to try and improve his finances, and further trips abroad to Germany in 1789 and 1790 failed to improve his position.

Despite these problems, Mozart's last years were to prove productive, with some of his most famous work, including *The Magic Flute*—with its Masonic overtones (Mozart had become a Freemason in 1784)—and his unfinished *Requiem* being produced in the year before his death on December 5, 1791. His death at the relatively early age of 35 has led to some debate as to the possible causes.

All Mozart's music is now numbered with a Köchel number, after Ludwig von Köchel who produced a comprehensive catalogue of the composer's works in 1862.

BEETHOVEN

"Keep your eye on him; one day he will make the world talk of him." Mozart in 1787, when Beethoven was 17

One of the most significant composers in history, Ludwig van Beethoven was the towering figure in western music during its transition from the Classical to the Romantic periods. He was born in Bonn on December 17, 1770, into a musical family; both his grandfather and father had been musicians employed by the Elector of Cologne, and his father was to be his first music teacher. Showing early talent, Beethoven was tutored from 1779 by Christian Gottlob Neefe, the recently appointed organist to the court and Bonn's leading musical teacher and who taught the young Beethoven musical composition.

From 1781—initially in an unpaid position, and from 1784 with a salary—Beethoven acted as Neefe's assistant organist and, in March 1783, with Neefe's help, his first compositions were published. Four years later Beethoven made a brief trip to Vienna in the hope of meeting Mozart; it is uncertain, however, whether the two ever met, although Beethoven's music was undoubtedly influenced by the older man. The visit was cut short by the death of his mother, and returning to Bonn, Beethoven had to cope not only with the loss of his mother but also the increasing alcoholism of his father, with the consequent need to help bring up his younger siblings.

Subsequently he became known to Count Ferdinand von Waldstein, who would be a leading patron to Beethoven during his career, while another influence was Joseph Haydn, who Beethoven first met in 1790 and who assisted with his studies following his move to Vienna in 1792.

Beethoven had initially intended to make a career as a piano player but under Haydn's tutelage he continued to study composition, also assisted by Antonio Salieri and Johann Albrechtsberger. Although his life in Vienna had

Left: Bonn university

originally been funded by the Elector of Cologne, this stipend ceased in the mid-1790s and thereafter Beethoven received support from a number of influential aristocrats while becoming established as a virtuoso performer on the piano.

Having spent much of 1794 in composing, Beethoven unveiled a number of significant pieces the following year, including the piano trios that became Opus 1. The success of these pieces brought Beethoven considerable fame and fortune, enabling him to undertake a major tour in 1796, visiting Prague, Dresden, Leipzig and Berlin, where his music was performed to considerable acclaim. During 1797, whilst back in Vienna, he suffered a serious illness and became aware for the first time of a slight deterioration in his hearing.

By 1802 he was aware that this deafness would ultimately become total. The deafness cause bouts of severe depression, particularly in later years, but he resolved to battle the disability, and the resulting works were amongst his greatest triumphs. However, following a failed attempt to perform his Piano Concerto No. 5 in 1811, he was eventually forced to give up performing in public, and despite the use of assorted hearing aids—many of which are now preserved—Beethoven was almost completely deaf by 1814.

From 1798, after a trip to Prague, he had devoted himself

Top left: Beethoven's music score for the last movement of the Ninth Symphony

Left: Willard White performs in a Royal Opera production of Beethoven's Fidelio.

"Through uninterrupted diligence you will receive Mozart's spirit through Haydn's hands." Count Ferdinand von Waldstein

increasingly to composition, tackling major orchestral works. His First and Second symphonies were completed in 1800 and 1802, as were six String Quartets, dedicated to his patron Prince Lobkowitz, between 1798 and 1800.

The first decade of the 19th century witnessed a transformation in Beethoven's musical style, becoming much more heroic in scale and power. This new approach was first demonstrated in his Third Symphony, *Eroica*, which was premièred in 1805. Lasting for 50 minutes, this was the longest symphony that had then been composed. This "middle" period of his career marked Beethoven's transition from a classical to a romantic composer, encompassing six of his nine symphonies along with the opera *Fidelio* and the Violin Concerto. But it was marred by increasing financial insecurity. He lost the position of composer in residence at the theater on the Wien River in Vienna in 1805, while ill health often forced him to spend time under medical supervision, and he also suffered failure in various romantic encounters.

These years were latterly marked by a decline in his artistic output until mid-1813 when news of Wellington's victory at Vitoria in Spain over the army of Napoleon encouraged him to write *Wellington's Victory*, which was premièred in Vienna in late 1813. The was to see the start of the third, or "late", phase of Beethoven's composing career, where the scale of the middle period was abandoned in favor of a much more intimate and lyrical style.

Inevitably, age and illness took their toll on Beethoven in his later years and there were periods after 1813 when little work was undertaken. Occasionally, however, there were periods when his health improved and he was able to continue to compose. It is during these years that two of his crowning triumphs–the *Choral* Symphony with its Ode to Joy (now used as the anthem of the European Union) and *Missa Solemnis*–were completed.

Increasingly bedridden through ill health, Beethoven died on March 26, 1827. His funeral, three days later, was witnessed by some 20,000 who lined the streets.

BEETHOVEN

BORN: December 17, 1770, in Bonn

DIED: March 26, 1827, in Vienna

INFLUENCED BY: Haydn, Mozart

INFLUENCED: Mendelssohn

KEY PIECES

Pathétique Piano Sonata (1799)

Symphony No. 1 (1800)

Prometheus (1801)

Moonlight Piano Sonata (1801)

Symphony No. 2 (1802)

Symphony No. 3 *Eroica* (1804)

Fidelio (1805)

Symphony No. 4 (1806)

Symphony No. 5 (1808)

Symphony No. 6 (1808)

Emperor Piano Concerto (1809)

Archduke Trio (1811)

Symphony No. 7 (1812)

Symphony No. 8 (1812)

Wellington's Victory (1813)

Symphony No. 9 *Choral* (1823)

Mass in D. *Missa Solemnis* (1823)

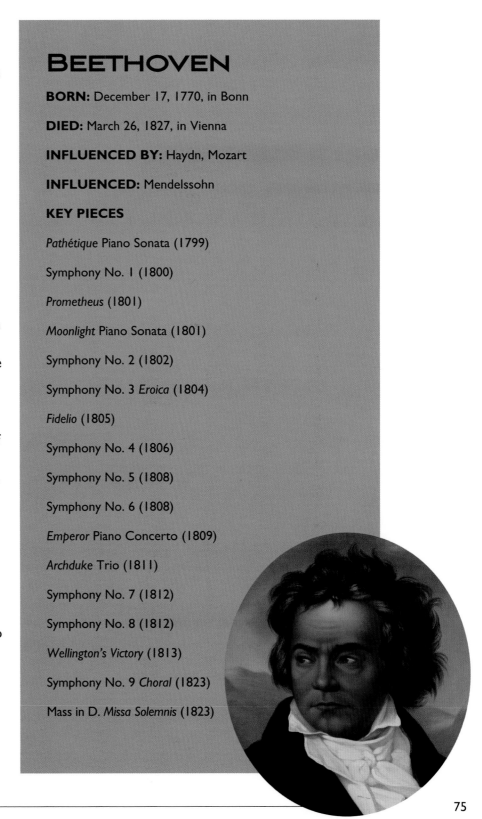

OTHER CLASSICAL COMPOSERS

• **Johann Albrechtsberger** *(1736-1809)* Austrian born and a close friend of Mozart, Albrechtsberger was one of the most important organists of the 18th century, as well as a prolific composer. As a teacher, one of his pupils was Ludwig van Beethoven.

• **Carl Philippe Emanuel Bach** *(1714-1788)* The son of Johann Sebastian Bach, C. P. E. Bach was a noted keyboard player and composer in his own right. He was influential in the development of the period of the sonata.

• **Johann Christian Bach** *(1735-1782)* Also a son of Johann Sebastian Bach, Johann Christian Bach was born in Germany but was based in England for much of his career, becoming known as "the London Bach". Music master to the family of King George III, he composed widely, with his work including symphonies and piano concertos.

• **Luigi Cherubini** *(1760-1842)* Born in Italy, but most successful during his years in Paris, Cherubini was a noted composer of opera, particularly towards the end of the 18th century. He was named by Beethoven as the greatest living composer.

Left: "Luigi Cherubini and the Lyric Muse" by Jean Auguste Dominique Ingres 1842

Far left: Johann Christian Bach

• **Muzio Clementi** *(1752-1832)* Although born in Italy, Clementi was based in Britain from 1774 and was one of the most prominent keyboard players of his age. Apart from his own compositions, he was also a piano maker and music publisher. His epitaph in Westminster Abbey calls him "The father of the pianoforte".

• **Christoph von Gluck** *(1714-1787)* Born in Germany but educated in Prague, von Gluck was one of the key figures in the development of opera in the 18th century. His major works include *Orfeo ed Euridice* of 1762.

• **Leopold Mozart** *(1719-1787)* Leopold Mozart, now better known as the father of Wolfgang Amadeus, was a court composer and violin teacher who wrote a significant number of both secular and religious pieces.

Above: Leopold Mozart

• **Antonio Salieri** *(1750-1825)* Italian born but based in Vienna for much of his life, Salieri was a highly influential composer of operas. Overshadowed by Mozart, the more lurid accusations about his involvement in the younger man's death are probably false.

Pages 78-79: The Berlin Philharmonic orchestra at the Requiem Mass for the late President Lech Kaczynski and his wife Maria in St. Mary's Basilica in Cracow, Poland, 18 April 2010

Above: Antonio Salieri

4 THE ROMANTIC ERA

"Every composer knows the anguish and despair occasioned by forgetting ideas which one has no time to write down."
Hector Berlioz

The composition of Beethoven's Symphony No. 7 in 1812 is often regarded as the start of the Romantic period in the early years of the 19th century—with Beethoven straddling it and the preceding classical period. Romanticism in music, which survived through until the early 20th century, is closely related to romanticism in the other arts, such as literature, painting and sculpture. The romantic movement believed that not all truth could be deduced from established principles but that there were inescapable realities that could only be appreciated through emotion, feeling and intuition.

The age was one of contradictions: a harkening back to the music of an earlier age combined with experimentation in terms of harmony and form. There were also new instruments to compose for and developments in earlier instruments that increased their range. Many composers of this era worked outside their discipline; both Schumann and Berlioz were noted writers and critics. Indeed, the former was influential in promoting the music of both Chopin and Brahms through the journal *Neue Zeitschrift für Musik (New Journal of Music)*. An awareness of landscape and nature, essential parts of the

Above: Paris Opera House
Right: Giuseppi Verdi conducting in Paris, 1880

romantic overview, played an important role in the work of many composers.

It was Felix Mendelssohn who, in 1840, revived Bach's great oratorio *St Matthew Passion*, and it was this revival that was at the core of the rediscovery of the "lost" music of earlier eras. This revival saw many composers, such as Brahms, deliberately and methodically exploring earlier music in their own compositions.

Another strand of considerable importance during the 19th century was nationalism, not only against the influence of the German-Austrian tradition of orchestral movement (which resulted in the creation of

Above: Robert Schumann

"national" schools of music in various countries, many of which again harkened back to the musical forms of those countries in earlier eras), but also against the great European empires–the Hapsburg and the Russian in particular–that dominated much of central and Eastern Europe.

It is perhaps no coincidence that the three great Scandinavian composers–Edvard Grieg in Norway, Carl Nielsen in Denmark and Jean Sibelius in Finland–were all rough contemporaries who grew up in an environment where their homelands were either ruled by another state or which had been recently defeated in war. Norway was under Swedish rule and would remain so until 1905; Denmark had been defeated by the combined armies of

Austria and Prussia in 1864 and had been forced to concede sovereignty over the north German provinces of Schleswig-Holstein; while Finland was to remain under ultimate Russian rule until 1917.

"After playing Chopin, I feel as if I had been weeping over sins that I had never committed, and mourning over tragedies that were not my own."
Oscar Wilde, 1891

Above: Caricature of Conductor Hector Berlioz by Grandville

Above: Franz Liszt conducting one of his oratorios in Budapest, with choir, orchestra and audience

The Romantic era was also marked by an increased domesticity—the piano, although developed in the late 17th or early 18th centuries, was becoming an instrument of choice for the homes of the growing numbers of the increasingly prosperous middle class throughout the continent. Family entertainment regularly involved piano playing, or singing accompanied by the piano, and most of the great Romantic composers produced small-scale pieces that were, and remain, central to the piano's repertoire. Moreover, many larger scale pieces were themselves transcribed for use by pianists.

The development of new instruments and the further modification of existing ones allowed for the further expansion—both in size and range—of the orchestra, whilst the modification to the traditional instruments allowed for soloists to demonstrate yet further virtuosity. Thus, the Romantic period also witnessed increasingly complex pieces that required skill, both on the part of the soloist and the orchestra. Improved musical education also brought a more sophisticated audience and a huge demand for concerts and other programs. Halls suitable for classical concerts were built in even relatively small towns and cities, and there was a massive growth in professional and amateur orchestras and choirs in many provincial centers. The Hallé Orchestra, Britain's oldest symphony orchestra was, for example, founded in Manchester by Charles Hallé in 1857.

The 19th century was also to witness a vast boom in the number of ballets and operas. Often with historical themes, these large-scale pieces remain the staple of opera houses and ballet companies worldwide.

However, ironically, the nationalist tendencies that had been at the core of the Romantic movement were also to prove its downfall. The optimism engendered by the late 19th century was to be destroyed irrevocably in the trenches of World War 1 and, after the war, new developments would see classical music enter the modern age.

MENDELSSOHN

"It was a Jew who restored this great Christian work to the public."
Mendelssohn on his promotion of Bach's St Matthew Passion

Straddling the Classical and Romantic eras, like Beethoven, and one of those who led the rediscovery of the music of Bach in the 19th century, (Jacob Ludwig) Felix Mendelssohn (-Bartholdy) was born in Hamburg on February 3, 1809. His grandfather was the Jewish philosopher Moses Mendelssohn, although his parents had abjured the faith and the composer was initially brought up without any religious influence. The family moved to Berlin in 1811, where Mendelssohn and his siblings were given the best education then available. When was about five, the family became Lutheran Christians at which time Felix also acquired the given names of Jacob and Ludwig. His father, Abraham, was a prosperous banker and, with the family's background, many of the leading

German intellectuals of the age were visitors to the family home. Among them was the poet Goethe who was to have a considerable influence on the intellectual development of the future composer when introduced to Mendelssohn by Friedrich Zelter in 1821.

Taking piano lessons from the age of six and studying in Paris under Marie Bigot the following year, Mendelssohn proved himself to be a prodigious talent and, in 1817, started to study composition under Zelter in Berlin. Zelter was an admirer of Johann Sebastian Bach and this undoubtedly influenced the musical development of the young Mendelssohn.

Above: Mendelssohn with his sister Fanny at the piano

Above: Mendelssohn playing before Queen Victoria

"I see as I write the smile with which Mendelssohn, whose enjoyment of Mlle. Lind's talent was unlimited, turned round and looked at me, as if a load of anxiety had been taken off his mind. His attachment to Mlle. Lind's genius as a singer was unbounded, as was his desire for her success."

A friend commenting on Mendelssohn's reaction watching Jenny Lind on stage in London in 1847

At the age of ten Mendelssohn gave his first public performance as a pianist, and started to compose significantly in adolescence. He wrote twelve string symphonies between the ages of twelve and fourteen; unlike much music written by children, these pieces are still regularly performed. His first published composition was a piano quartet written when he was thirteen but his first truly significant work was his String Octet completed when he was sixteen. The overture *A Midsummer's Night Dream*, which includes the famous Wedding March, was completed when he was seventeen.

Apart from his musical skill, Mendelssohn was also a noted linguist–speaking English, Italian and Latin as well as his native German–and a highly proficient artist, particularly in watercolors. He completed his formal education at the University of Berlin, where he studied from 1826 to 1829, and in his final year the 20-year-old Mendelssohn conducted Johann Sebastian Bach's magnificent *St Matthew Passion* in Berlin, the first performance of the piece since its composer's death in 1750. The success of the performance helped to seal Mendelssohn's reputation and spark the revival of interest in Bach's music.

In 1833, following the death of Zelter the previous year, Mendelssohn had hopes of replacing his mentor as the conductor of the Berlin Singakademie; he was, however, overlooked. This was possibly due to his youth or to his Jewish antecedents. For a while he divided his

Above: Fingal's Cave

time between trips to Britain—a country that he visited no fewer than ten times after his first visit in 1829 and which inspired two of his most famous pieces, the *Hebrides Overture* (better known as *Fingal's Cave*) and the *Scottish Symphony*—and Düsseldorf, where he was appointed musical director in 1833.

He spent nearly twenty months in Britain between 1829 and 1847, and during that time he assisted British music through the editing of new editions of the music of composers such as Handel and Bach, whilst also conducting both his and other composers' music. It was in Birmingham that his late great oratorio *Elijah* was to receive its world première on August 26, 1846.

His next appointment was as conductor of the Leipzig Gewandhaus Orchestra. He played a significant role in the musical development of the city, including giving a première to his oratorio *St Paul*, a piece completed shortly after the death of his father, in 1836. The following year Mendelssohn married Cécile Jeanrenaud, the daughter of a French Protestant clergyman, and they were to have five children between then and 1844. In 1844 he met the Swedish soprano Jenny Lind, although the extent of their relationship is still shrouded in some mystery.

In 1841 Mendelssohn had moved back to Berlin at the invitation of the new king Friedrich Wilhelm IV, who was keen to see the city develop as a musical and cultural center. His sojourn in Berlin was, however, short-lived, although he did compose some church music whilst based there. In 1843 he returned to Leipzig where he founded the Leipzig Conservatory and where he was to live until his early death on November 4, 1847.

MENDELSSOHN

BORN: February 3, 1809, in Hamburg

DIED: November 4, 1847, in Leipzig

INFLUENCED BY: Bach, Mozart, Beethoven

KEY PIECES

Symphony No. 1 (1824)

A Midsummer's Night Dream (1826)

Hebrides Overture (1830)

Symphony No. 3 (Scottish) (1842)

St Paul (1836)

Elijah (1846)

BRAHMS

"Without craftsmanship, inspiration is a mere reed shaken in the wind."
Brahms

One of the most influential of the composers of the Romantic period, Johannes Brahms was born in Hamburg on May 7, 1833. His father was a professional musician who had moved to the city in order to further his career. His mother, seventeen years older than his father, was 44 when the composer was born.

Showing a talent for music from an early age, Brahms was initially tutored by his father, although he was also to study the piano under Otto Friedrich Willibald Cossel, and then with Eduard Marxsen and Carl Maria von Bocklet. However, the family's financial position was not strong, and from a relatively early age Brahms supplemented the family income by playing the piano in dockside taverns and brothels. His reputation as a musician grew and, at the age of 19, he made his first concert tour, during which he met the violinist Joseph Joachim and the composer Franz Liszt. Brahms's relationship with the latter was, however, slightly

Above: Brahm's birthplace, Hamburg

Above: Brahms takes tea

Above: Interior of Brahms' house in Vienna

tarnished when he fell asleep during a performance of Liszt's Sonata in B Minor!

It was Joachim who gave the young Brahms a letter of introduction to Robert Schumann in Düsseldorf, and it was Schumann who announced the arrival of a prodigious new talent in an article published in *Neue Zeitschrift für Musik (New Journal of Music)*. Whilst with the Schumann family, Brahms became close with the older man's wife, Clara, and their children. Whilst the extent of the relationship between Clara and Brahms is uncertain, the latter took care of the family after the death of Schumann, who had been confined to a lunatic asylum in 1854. Although engaged for a period to Agathe von Siebold in 1859, Brahms was destined to remain unmarried.

Whilst Brahms had experimented with composition from his childhood, these early works were destroyed, and it is only from the late 1850s that he commenced a career in composition. It was his mother's death in 1865–three years after Brahms had first visited Vienna, a city that was to become his permanent home in 1863–that was to lead to the composition of his first major work, *Ein Deutches Requiem*, which was to receive its first full performance in 1868 in Bremen.

It was the success of this piece that established Brahms's reputation as a leading composer and led to two decades of considerable success that encompassed the production of four symphonies and much chamber music. Although he had decided to retire from composition in 1890, he was inspired to compose a number of final pieces, including four for the noted clarinetist Richard Mühlfeld–the Clarinet Trio, the Clarinet Quintet and two Clarinet Sonatas–prior to his death in Vienna on April 3,1897.

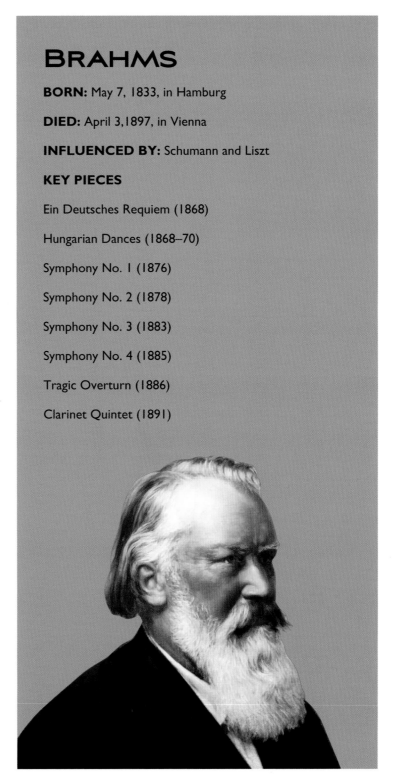

BRAHMS

BORN: May 7, 1833, in Hamburg

DIED: April 3,1897, in Vienna

INFLUENCED BY: Schumann and Liszt

KEY PIECES

Ein Deutsches Requiem (1868)

Hungarian Dances (1868–70)

Symphony No. 1 (1876)

Symphony No. 2 (1878)

Symphony No. 3 (1883)

Symphony No. 4 (1885)

Tragic Overturn (1886)

Clarinet Quintet (1891)

TCHAIKOVSKY

"I am Russian in the most complete possible sense of that word."

Tchaikovsky, in a letter to Madame Nadezhda von Meck in 1878

One of the 19th century's major composers of ballet and opera music, Pyotr Ilyich (Peter Ilich) Tchaikovsky was born in Kamsko-Votkinsk, in the Ural Mountains, on May 7, 1840, into a middle-class family. His parents had aspirations that he would take up a career as a civil servant, despite his evident talent for music. Choosing to ignore his family, he entered the conservatory at St Petersburg in 1862 after a period studying at law school and a brief career in the Ministry of Justice. It was whilst he was studying law that his mother died in 1854, an event that was to haunt the future composer for the rest of his life.

After three years at the conservatory, he moved to Moscow to join Nicholas Rubinstein, his teacher of orchestration, to himself teach harmony at the conservatory that had opened in 1866. Combining teaching with composition, Tchaikovsky's reputation increased as pieces such as *Swan Lake* and *Eugene Onegin* received their premières. Despite the success that his music was bringing, the composer himself was personally insecure. Despite being homosexual by inclination, he married one of his pupils—Antonina Ivanovna Milyukova—in 1877, although the marriage was never consummated and Tchaikovsky fled after a month in a state of nervous collapse. (He

Above: St Petersburg

remained married until his death in 1893, despite a fraught relationship with his wife.)

Traveling initially to Switzerland for recuperation, in the years after his return to Russia in 1879 he continued to compose whilst leading an itinerant life. It was during this time that he was put into contact with Nadezhda von Meck, the widow of a railway magnate, who became the composer's patron and confidante. The two were to correspond regularly over the next thirteen years, although they never actually met. Despite becoming related by marriage—one of her sons married the composer's niece—communication ceased in 1890 due to her increasing financial worries. The

Above: The Royal Ballet in a production of The Nutcracker *at the Royal Opera House, Covent Garden, London*

Right: Nadezhda von Meck Nadezdha who championed the music of Tchaikovsky

loss of his patron, although no longer necessary financially, was to affect Tchaikovsky significantly.

In 1880 Tchaikovsky was commissioned to compose one of the pieces for which he is perhaps best known. The *1812 Overture* was designed to mark the 70th anniversary of Napoleon's disastrous assault on Moscow and his ignominious retreat westwards. Not one of the composer's personal favorites of his own work, the overture remains one of the most popular pieces of classical music. The commission from Tsar Alexander II, who died in 1881 to be succeeded by Alexander III, also brought the composer public rewards, such as the Order of St Vladimir in 1884, which helped Tchaikovsky re-establish himself in society. The next decade, prior to his death on November 6,1893, saw his international status grow and his final compositions.

"There is something so special about our relationship that it often stops me in my tracks with amazement. I have told you more than once, I believe, that you have come to seem to me the hand of Fate itself, watching over me and protecting me. The very fact that I do not know you personally, while feeling so close to you, accords you in my eyes the special status of an unseen but benevolent presence, like a benign Providence."

Tchaikovsky, to Madame Nadezhda von Meck, explaining her importance to him

TCHAIKOVSKY

BORN: May 7, 1840, in Kamsko-Votkinsk, Russia

DIED: November 6, 1893, in St Petersburg

INFLUENCED: Glinka, Rimsky-Korsakov, Mussorgsky

KEY PIECES

Swan Lake (1877; revised 1895)

Eugene Onegin (1878)

1812 Overture (1880)

The Sleeping Beauty (1890)

Nutcracker (1892)

WAGNER

*"If one has not heard Wagner at Bayreuth,
one has heard nothing!"*
Gabriel Fauré, 1884

One of the greatest of all opera composers, and one of the most significant of the romantics of the 19th century, (Wilhelm) Richard Wagner was born in Leipzig, the son of a clerk in the local police, on May 22, 1813. His father died six months later and, following his mother's remarriage to the actor and playwright Ludwig Geyer, the family moved to Dresden the following year. Educated initially in Dresden and later—after the death of his step-father in 1821 and the family's return to the town of his birth in 1827—in Leipzig, Wagner showed an early aptitude for music and from 1828 started to receive lessons in musical composition. His education was concluded by study at the University of Leipzig from 1831, with further musical study under Christian Theodor Weinlig, cantor of St Thomas's Church, who was so impressed by Wagner's skill that he refused payment for the tuition.

In 1833 Wagner became choirmaster at Würzburg and completed his first opera, *Die Feen (The Fairies)* in the same year; this piece was, however, not to be performed during his lifetime. In 1834 Wagner became musical director of the Magdeburg Opera, leading to the first performance of his second opera—*Das Liebesverbot (The Ban on Love* based on Shakespeare's *Measure for Measure)*—but the collapse of the Magdeburg Opera financially left Wagner in a precarious financial position. Debt would be one of Wagner's problems throughout his life, and he was forced to flee Riga in 1839 as a result of the debts incurred by himself and his wife of three years, Christine Wilhelmine "Minna" Planer.

Above: Leipzig, Wagner's birthplace

Above: Bayreuth theater

Above: Opera soprano Lillian Nordica, best known for her performances in Wagner operas, in costume as Brünnhilde in Die Walküre

Following a brief trip to London—in which the rough sea crossing inspired *Die Fliegende Holländer (The Flying Dutchman)*—the Wagners moved to Paris, living there until 1842 when they moved back to Dresden, where *The Flying Dutchman* and *Tannhäuser* received their premières. However, in 1849 Wagner moved again, as a result of his support for the May uprising against King Frederick Augustus II of Saxony. Wagner and his wife were to spend the next twelve years in exile in Paris and Zurich, with financial support coming from Franz Liszt, during which time *Lohengrin*, first performed by Liszt at Weimar in 1850, was completed along with the first elements of what became the "Ring" cycle.

In 1861, Wagner was permitted to return to Germany and settled for a while in Biebrich in Prussia. Life, however, remained a struggle until he received the patronage of King Ludwig II of Bavaria, who brought the composer to Munich and settled his debts. The result of the patronage was to see the première of *Tristan und Isolde* in 1865, the first of Wagner's operas to be premièred since *Lohengrin*. During this time, Wagner commenced his affair with Cosima von Bülow, the

"Wagner has wonderful moments, and dreadful quarters of an hour."
Gioachino Rossini

"One of the most beautiful friendships of my life."
Wagner, referring in his autobiography to his friendship with Samuel Lehrs, a Jew, during his years in Paris

WAGNER

BORN: May 22 ,1813, in Leipzig

DIED: February 13, 1883, in Venice

INSPIRED BY: Beethoven

INSPIRED: Elgar

KEY PIECES

Der Fliegende Holländer (The Flying Dutchman) (1843)

Tannhäuser (1845)

Lohengrin (1850)

Der Ring des Nibelungen (The Ring Cycle comprising *Das Rheingold [The Rhinegold], Die Walküre [The Valkyrie], Siegfried* and *Götterdämmerung [The Twilight of the Gods]*)

Tristan und Isolde (1865)

Parsifal (1882)

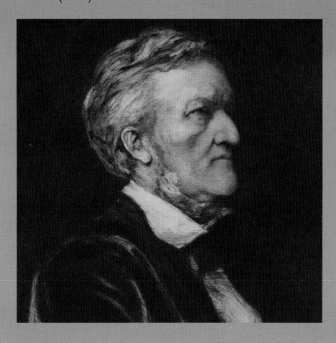

illegitimate daughter of Franz Liszt. The two were to be married in 1870 following the death of Wagner's wife Minna and the von Bülows' divorce.

The Bavarian establishment disapproved of Wagner's influence on Ludwig and, in December 1865, the composer was once again forced into exile in Switzerland, where he continued to compose. It was whilst in Switzerland, in 1871, that Wagner decided to construct a new opera house at Bayreuth, moving to the town in 1872. Fundraising for the new theater took a considerable time, although once again Wagner was aided considerably by the generosity of King Ludwig. The *Festspielhaus* (Festival Theater) was completed in 1876 and opened with the première of the Ring cycle. The Bayreuth Festival continues to be held annually, celebrating Wagner's music.

Much of Wagner's later years were spent in Italy where he completed his final opera, *Parsifal*, in 1882; he died on February 13, 1883, in Venice. Wagner's reputation has suffered significantly over the past century, largely as a result of his anti-Semitism—although he did have numerous Jewish friends—and his post-mortem association with Adolf Hitler and the Nazi regime in Germany after 1933.

MAHLER

"A symphony must be like the world. It must contain everything."
Gustav Mahler

Largely known as a conductor during his own lifetime, Gustav Mahler, an Austrian-born Jew (his faith was to cause him problems as he aspired to climb the musical hierarchy in Vienna), was to compose only eighteen pieces. But these works include ten symphonies that have become, since his death, recognized as among the most important to be composed in the thirty years leading up to World War 1.

Above: Gustav Mahler and his wife Alma taking a walk nearby their summer residence in Toblach

MAHLER

BORN: July 7, 1860, in Kalischt, Bohemia

DIED: May 18, 1911, in Vienna

INSPIRED BY: Beethoven and Liszt

INSPIRED: Schoenberg

KEY PIECES

First four symphonies (1889-1901)

Lieder eines fahrenden Gesellen (1896)

Choral *Eighth Symphony* (1906)

Das Lied von der Erde (1909)

Ninth Symphony (1909)

SCINTTO
Photo

PUCCINI

"Inspiration is an awakening, a quickening of all man's faculties, and it is manifested in all high artistic achievements."
Giacomo Puccini

Possibly the last great composer of opera from Italy in the tradition of Rossini and Verdi, Giacomo Puccini spent most of his life at Torre del Lago, not far from where he was born. There he composed his greatest works, but his life was not without controversy. In 1909 a scandal ensued after Elvira, his wife, accused their maid of conducting an affair with her husband. The maid was driven to suicide, and her family successfully sued Elvira. He moved to Viareggio in 1921 forced out of his home by industrial pollution. His body was taken there after his death and a chapel was created in the villa where he and other family members are buried. The annual Festival Puccini takes place close to the villa.

Above: Madame Butterfly *by Puccini*

PUCCINI

BORN: December 22, 1858, in Lucca

DIED: November 29, 1924, in Paris

INSPIRED BY: Verdi and Wagner

KEY PIECES

La bohème (1896)

Tosca (1900)

Madame Butterfly (1904)

Turandot (1924)

RACHMANINOV

"Music is enough for a lifetime, but a lifetime is not enough for music."
Sergei Rachmaninov

The last great Russian composer of the Romantic era, most of Rachmaninovs music was composed before he was forced to flee his homeland after the 1917 Russian Revolution. After this he completed fewer than ten pieces, spending most of his time performing—when he first arrived in New York in 1918 he played forty concerts in four months. He composed both sacred and secular music and was a notably brilliant pianist. A friend and mentor of Vladimir Horowitz, Rachmaninov became an American citizen in 1943 and was buried at Kensico Cemetery in Valhalla, New York following his death from melanoma.

Above: Rachmaninov driving a car.

RACHMANINOV

BORN: April 1, 1873, in Semyonovo, NW Russia

DIED: March 28, 1943, in Beverly Hills, CA

INSPIRED BY: Tchaikovsky

INSPIRED: Horowitz

KEY PIECES

Prelude in C# Minor (1892)

Piano Concerto No. 2 (1901)

Piano Concerto No. 3 (1909)

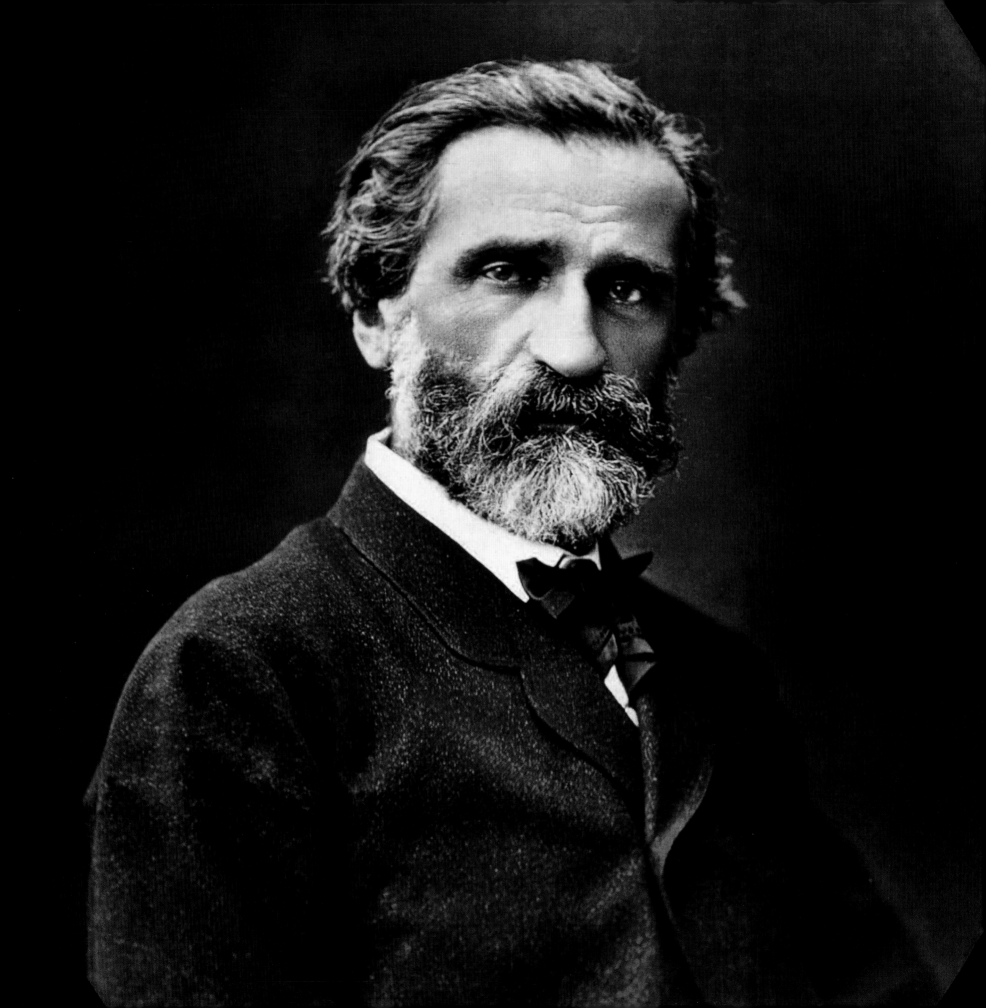

VERDI

"Stupid criticism and still more stupid praise."
Giuseppe Verdi, speaking of the press notices of Aïda

Perhaps the dominant Italian composer of operas in the late 19th century, Verdi's works have stood the test of time and are among the most beloved of opera audiences worldwide. He was not an immediate success: his first opera *Oberto* went down well but his second was unsuccessful–probably as a result of the death of his wife during the composition. Everything changed with Nabucco and he went on to compose many great operas, including *Un ballo in maschera* (1859) and *La forza del destino* (1861).

Verdi was said to have played a significant role in the Risorgimento-the unification of Italy. He certainly became a member of the Chamber of Deputies in 1861, but his political influence is almost certainly overstated.

Above: La Traviata *by Verdi*

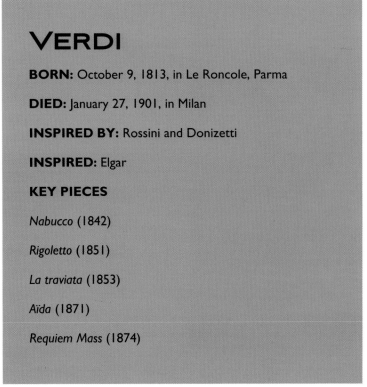

VERDI

BORN: October 9, 1813, in Le Roncole, Parma

DIED: January 27, 1901, in Milan

INSPIRED BY: Rossini and Donizetti

INSPIRED: Elgar

KEY PIECES

Nabucco (1842)

Rigoletto (1851)

La traviata (1853)

Aïda (1871)

Requiem Mass (1874)

OTHER ROMANTIC COMPOSERS

• **Hector Berlioz** *(1803–1869)* The French composer Berlioz was one of the first composers to emerge who was not a virtuoso on a particular instrument. He was, however, to become a well-known conductor and musical critic. He composed four symphonies and five operas, as well as other orchestral and vocal pieces. His best-known work is perhaps his *Symphonie Fantastique* (1830).

• **Anton Bruckner** *(1824–1896)* Born in Austria, Bruckner composed a relatively small number of pieces–less than forty in all–but these included ten symphonies, and he was important in the development of this type of music during the 19th century. Strongly religious, Bruckner's works also include a number of significant choral works, including his *Requiem Mass* (1848).

• **Frédéric Chopin** *(1810–1849)* Polish-born Chopin, exiled from his homeland in 1831, was one of the greatest of pianists and one of the most important composers of music for the piano. Out of almost 220 compositions, more than 190 were for the piano. His works include *Barcarolle* (1846), which was his last major composition.

Above: Frédéric Chopin

• **Claude Debussy** *(1862–1918)* One of the key figures in the transition from Romantic to Modern classical music, the French-born Debussy was a pioneer in adopting the ideas engendered by Impressionism into music. Amongst his best-known works is *La Mer (The Sea)* of 1905.

• **Antonín Dvořák** *(1841–1904)* A Czech nationalist, Dvořák studied the folk music tradition of homeland widely, which he incorporated into his compositions. Spending some years in the USA, his best-known piece is perhaps his Symphony No. 9 *From the New World*.

• **Edvard Grieg** *(1843–1907)* Born in Norway, Grieg's musical style was developed through his close study of local folk music and traditions. His best-known pieces are probably the two *Peer Gynt Suites*, which were based around a Norwegian fairy story.

Above: Anton Bruckner

• **Franz Liszt** *(1811–1886)* One of the most important figures in the Romantic movement, Liszt was born in Hungary. A noted pianist, composer (of which more than 500 pieces of the almost 750 works he completed were for the piano), teacher and promoter, Liszt's works include his Piano Concerto No. 1 (1855).

• **Carl Nielsen** *(1865–1931)* Hailing from Denmark, Nielsen was one of the most important symphonic composers of the early 20th century, but he also composed operas and other pieces. His most popular work is probably his Symphony No. 4 *The Inextinguishable*.

• **Giachino Rossini** *(1792–1868)* Probably the greatest composer of opera in the first half of the 19th century, works by the Italian-born composer include *Il Barbiere di Siviglia (The Barber of Seville)* of 1816 and *Guillaume Tell (William Tell)* of 1829.

• **Franz Schubert** *(1797–1828)* Destined to have a short life through ill-health, Franz Schubert was born in Austria and studied, like Beethoven, under Salieri in Vienna. He composed nine symphonies—including his famous No. 8 *Unfinished*—as well as other orchestral pieces, operas, choral pieces and songs.

• **Jean Sibelius** *(1865–1957)* One of the most important symphonic composers of the early 20th century, Sibelius was born in Finland at a time when his homeland was ruled by Russia. As a result, there's a strong nationalistic streak in much of his music—such as *Karelia Suite* (1893) and *Finlandia* (1899).

Above: Caricature statue of Giachino Rossini

Above: Richard Strauss poster, 1910

• **Johann Strauss** *(1804–1849)* The father of a musical dynasty that was to be hugely influential in the development of the waltz. His most famous work is probably the *Radetzky March* that was composed in 1848 to mark the Austrian army's victory over an Italian uprising.

• **Richard Strauss** *(1864–1949)* Unrelated to the Austrian Strauss family, Richard Strauss was born in Germany and was to compose orchestral pieces, operas, ballets and song cycles. Unfortunately, his later career was tainted by his association with the Nazi Party under the Third Reich. One of his pieces, the tone poem *Also Sprach Zarathustra (Thus Spoke Zoroaster)*, was used in the classic Stanley Kubrick film *2001: A Space Odyssey*.

• **Ralph Vaughan Williams** *(1872–1958)* One of the most important British composers of the 20th century, Vaughan Williams composed nine symphonies and eleven operas, more than twenty choral pieces and a number of other orchestral pieces. His most familiar work is probably *Fantasia on a Theme by Thomas Tallis*, which he composed in 1910 and revised thirteen years later.

5 MODERN MUSIC

"My music is not modern it is merely badly played."
Arnold Schoenberg

The history of classical music is arguably much more complex than that for any other period of history. As with art and other forms of culture, the years since 1900 have been marked by a great variety of disparate strands and influences. Major factors in the development of classical music have included political ideologies, technological developments and an increasing awareness of historic music and instruments. The growth of popular media such as radio, television, films and advertising has made music much more familiar and more readily available than it has ever been in the past. One element of the development of music has been the rise of dissonance as opposed to consonance—the pleasing effect of a chord—which emerged as a trend from the late 19th century. This led to the description of the 20th century as the "dissonant period" of classical music.

At the start of the century there was a number of composers—Sibelius in Finland and Mahler in Austria, for example—who were exponents of the Romantic style of composition. Drawing upon the Austro-German Romantic tradition was Arnold Schoenberg whose relationship with Expressionist painters like Kandinsky and Kokoschka led him to develop Expressionist themes in music. Schoenberg's "free atonal" period, from 1908 to 1921, was perhaps the height of this particular style of music, with his pupils Alban Berg and Anton Webern also producing music in this style.

Other composers, such as Mahler, Bartók, Hindemath and Ives, also demonstrated Expressionist traits in some of their

Above: Arnold Schoenberg

compositions. Expressionism, however, was largely in decline by the late 1920s, largely as a result of the rise of neoclassicism. Despised as degenerate art by Nazi Germany, Expressionism found renewed favor amongst composers after 1945.

One of the earliest reactions against the Romantic era was to be found in France where Claude Debussy spearheaded the use of Impressionism within musical composition. It was an assault upon the emotional exuberance and epic themes evinced in the German Romantic tradition, particularly for example in the music of Wagner, in favor of art as a sensuous experience, rather than an ethical or intellectual one. He argued for the

Right: Claude Debussy

"Music is given to us with the sole purpose of establishing an order in things, including, and particularly, the co–ordination between man and time."
Igor Stravinsky

Above: Igor Stravinsky

composers drew inspiration. The term is used for music that revived earlier instruments, practices and techniques. Notable exponents of this type of music were Igor Stravinsky, with pieces such as *Pulcinella* (1918) and *The Rake's Progress* (1948–51); Sergei Prokofiev, with his *Classical Symphony* (Symphony No. 1 of 1917); and Maurice Ravel, with *Le tombeau de Couperin* (1917–19). In Britain, Ralph Vaughan Williams was another composer who explored historical music, most notably in his haunting *Fantasia on a Theme by Thomas Tallis*, which was originally composed in 1910 and revised thirteen years later.

Williams, however, was not a neoclassicist but was a composer that evinced another of the great strands of 20th century composition: the awareness of a nation's musical heritage, both classical and folk. Williams himself composed workings of traditional folk songs, and he was not alone in this. Both Béla Bartók and Zoltán Kodály traveled widely through central Europe collecting recordings of folk tunes that they incorporated into their work, whilst Percy Grainger, who was Australian born but lived most of his career in Europe and North America, also made extensive records of folk tunes, many of which he incorporated into his own compositions. In North America, Aaron Copland explored the heritage of the music of the cowboys and nonconformists in his work.

The history of music in the 20th century cannot be divorced from the two powerful political movements of the era—Communism and Fascism—just as music of the 16th century was heavily influenced by the Reformation and Counter-Reformation. The Nazi regime in Germany banned the work of Jewish composers, such as Alban Berg, in favor of promoting the works of the German romantics, most notably Wagner, that helped to foster the myth of the Third Reich. In Soviet Russia composers such as Shostakovich were forced to compose in an environment where the state was dominant; it was only after the collapse of the Soviet system and the liberation of the states of eastern Europe that composers such as Arvo Pärt were able to give full expression to their music.

rediscovery of the work of the masters of the 18th century for whom music had been a route to charm and entertain. Apart from Debussy, other noted composers of the Impressionist school included Maurice Ravel, Frederick Delius, Ottorino Respighi and Paul Dukas. Although again largely overtaken by neoclassicism by the late 1920s, traits of Impressionism can be found throughout the music of the 20th century.

Neoclassicism was a throwback, as its name suggests, to the music of the 17th and 18th centuries from which

Above: Aaron Copland

If there was one dominant theme of modern classical music it is perhaps experimentation. Following Schoenberg's period of atonality, for example, he developed the 12-tone technique. But this represented a development of composition using traditional instruments; more recently composers have been able to adopt electronic devices and instruments. The era is littered with phrases such as "modernism", "postmodernism" and "minimalism" as classical music responds to the world in as many different ways as the other arts. Works such as John Cage's postmodern 4'3"–in which there is complete silence as the instruments are instructed *not* to play during the piece's duration–show that, with classical music in the contemporary age, there are virtually no bounds.

Above: Nancy Maultsby and American Robert Swensen perform in the opera Oedipus Rex *by Igor Stravinsky and Jean Cocteau*

ELGAR

"There is music in the air. All you have to do is take as much as you require."
Elgar

Born in the English Worcestershire village of Lower Broadheath on June 2, 1857, Edward Elgar was the son of William Elgar, an organist and music dealer. His mother, Anne, had converted to Catholicism shortly before the composer's birth, and so he was raised in the Catholic faith—an irony, considering how prominent a role he fulfilled in the Protestant establishment, and the music that he wrote for the great state occasions and for use by the Anglican communion.

Growing up in the Malvern Hills, an area to which he remained emotionally attached throughout his life and to which he returned regularly, Elgar was not formally trained as a musician but was largely self-taught. However, he hoped to study music in Leipzig at the age of 15 but the family's financial position precluded this and he left school and started work with a local solicitor. Music, however, remained his first love and his legal career was cut short when he took the decision to pursue his vocation.

Initially giving piano and violin lessons, he also worked in his father's shop. Involved with the Worcester Glee Club, one of a number of local musical societies that existed at the time that

Above: Elgar's birthplace museum in Worcestershire, England

encouraged the singing of short songs, Elgar was appointed bandmaster at the Worcester & County Lunatic Asylum when he was 22 and also succeeded his father as the organist of St George's RC church in Worcester. As a violinist he also played with orchestras in local musical festivals, playing on one occasion in a concert conducted by Dvořák. It was at this time that he also arranged pieces of music by composers such as Beethoven for use by a wind quintet and his friends. Through this he gradually improved his compositional and arrangement skills—competence that would stand him in good stead once his own career as a composer developed.

Above: Elgar at a recording of the Nursery Suite *in the presence of the Duke and Duchess of York in 1931*

In 1880 he made the first of his trips abroad and came into contact with the quality of music being composed in Europe at the time, most notably that of Richard Wagner. Although he was married in 1889–to Caroline Roberts, the daughter of Major-General Sir Henry Roberts (whose family considered Elgar socially unsuitable)–the 1880s were a decade of despondency for the aspiring composer as he sought recognition. A move to London proved unsuccessful, but it was the return to Great Malvern, where he could earn a living as a music teacher and conductor, that was to see Elgar start to achieve considerable success. In 1890, the Elgars' only child, a daughter, was born.

During the 1890s he started to compose works for the great choral festivals of the English Midlands, most notably the Three Choirs Festival (based on the three cathedrals of Gloucester, Hereford and Worcester), and this was to see his reputation gradually established. It was, however, his first major orchestral piece–the *Enigma Variations* of 1899–that made his name. This was followed in 1900 by the choral piece *The Dream of Gerontius*. Elgar's position was secured in 1902 when he composed much of the music performed at the coronation of King Edward VII; this included the music, with words by A. C. Benson, for *Land of Hope and Glory*. In 1904 Elgar was knighted, one of many awards that he was to achieve during the final thirty years of his life.

In the years leading up to the outbreak of World War 1, Elgar had great success, composing, amongst other pieces, his two symphonies and the violin and cello concertos. Post-war, however, his popularity declined, although he was appointed Master of the King's Musick in 1924. During these years, however, he was one of the first composers to grasp enthusiastically the new medium of recorded music, and he was to conduct performances of many of his own compositions for the Gramophone Company. He continued to compose during the final decade of his life; however, several pieces, most notably his Third Symphony, were left incomplete when he died in 1934.

"I have sketched a set of Variations on an original theme. The Variations have amused me because I've labelled them with the nicknames of my particular friends... that is to say I've written the variations each one to represent the mood of the "party" (the person)... and have written what I think they would have written–if they were asses enough to compose."
Elgar

ELGAR

BORN: June 2, 1857, in Lower Broadheath, Worcestershire, England

DIED: February 23, 1934, in Worcester, England

INSPIRED BY: Wagner

KEY PIECES

Enigma Variations (1899)

The Dream of Gerontius (1900)

Symphony No. 1 (1907–08)

Violin Concerto (1909–10)

Symphony No. 2 (1909–1911)

Pomp & Circumstance Marches (1901–30)

Cello Concerto (1918–19)

Symphony No. 3 (1932–34; unfinished)

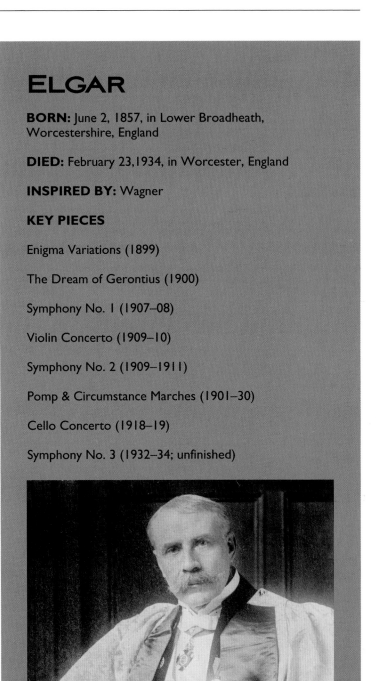

BRITTEN

"A subject very close to my heart–the struggle of the individual against the masses. The more vicious the society, the more vicious the individual."
Benjamin Britten on Peter Grimes *in 1948*

Undoubtedly the most influential British composer of the late 20th century, (Edward) Benjamin Britten was born in Lowestoft, on the English Suffolk coast, the son of a dentist, on November 22, 1913. His father was a keen amateur musician and Benjamin was to demonstrate a gift for music from an early age. Alongside his conventional education, Britten started to study music with the composer Frank Bridge at the age of 11. Britten subsequently studied at the Royal College of Music under John Ireland and was also to be influenced by another great British composer of the mid–10th century, Ralph Vaughan Williams. A planned trip to Austria, to study under Alban Berg, in 1935 was thwarted by his parents who believed that Berg would prove a bad influence.

In 1935 he was invited by the director Alberto Cavalcantii to become involved with the growing documentary film movement in England. Working with the GPO Film Unit and with the poet W. H. Auden, Britten's work at this time included the music for the classic film *Night Mail*. In 1937 Britten met the tenor, Peter Pears, who was to become Britten's life-long partner and collaborator of much of the composer's work.

Shortly before the outbreak of World War 2, Britten and Pears traveled to the United States, where

Above: Snape Maltings concert hall

they were to spend three years prior to returning to Britain. Two of Britten's more important early works–*Hymn to St Cecilia* and *A Ceremony of Carols*–were completed on the voyage home. On their return to the United Kingdom, both Britten and Pears registered as conscientious objectors. At the same time, work had started on his opera *Billy Budd*, which was to receive its première in 1945. There was, however, some resistance within the British musical establishment to Britten and this led him, in 1947, to establish the

English National Opera and, in 1948 (having moved with Pears to Aldeburgh in 1945), the Aldeburgh Festival.

Based at Aldeburgh for the rest of his life, Britten continued to compose both orchestral and operatic pieces. Amongst the orchestral music that he composed were a number of cello pieces for the noted Russian cellist Mstislav Rostropovich, with whom Britten became acquainted in the 1960. He also became friends with the Russian composer Dmitri Shostakovich, who dedicated his Fourteenth Symphony to Britten and to whom Britten had dedicated *The Prodigal Son*. Probably Britten's greatest success of the 1960s was, however, his *War Requiem*, which was composed to mark the consecration of the new Coventry Cathedral in 1962.

Receiving numerous honors–Britten became a Companion of Honour in 1953 and received the Order of Merit in 1965–the composer had turned down a knighthood prior to being awarded a life peerage in 1976.

Above: A dress rehearsal of Benjamin Britten's opera Death in Venice *in Bregenz, 2007*

Above: Sir Peter Pears

Already ill, however, Britten was to die on December 4, 1976. He is buried in the churchyard of St Peter and St Paul in Aldeburgh, alongside the grave of Sir Peter Pears (who died in 1986). A complex figure, Britten's undoubted reputation as a composer is often overshadowed by his personality. Not only homosexual at a time when, and for most of his life, such activity was illegal in Britain, he was also notoriously attracted to youngsters, including the actor David Hemmings, although suggestions of impropriety were few.

With the benefit of hindsight, it is perhaps significant that the last great opera he composed—*Death in Venice*—is based upon a novella written by the German author Thomas Mann that tells the story of a doomed relationship between an artist—a writer in the original book—and a teenage boy.

"My subject is War, and the pity of War.
The Poetry is in the pity...
All a poet can do today is warn."
Wilfred Owen, quoted by Benjamin Britten on the title page to the score of War Requiem *1962*

BRITTEN

BORN: November 22, 1913, in Lowestoft, England

DIED: December 4, 1976, in Aldeburgh, England

INFLUENCED BY: Frank Bridge, John Ireland, Ralph Vaughan Williams

INFLUENCED: Arvo Pärt

KEY PIECES

Variation on a Theme of Frank Bridge (1937)

Hymn to St Cecilia (1942)

A Ceremony of Carols (1942)

Peter Grimes (1945)

Young Person's Guide to the Orchestra (1946)

Albert Herring (1947)

Billy Budd (1951)

Noye's Fludde (1957)

Turn of the Screw (1954)

A Midsummer's Night Dream (1960)

War Requiem (1962)

Death in Venice (1973)

PÄRT

"He just seemed to shake his sleeves and notes would fall out."

Comment on Pärt whilst he was studying at the Tallinn Conservatory in 1957

Born on September 11, 1935, in Paide, then part of the independent Baltic Republic of Estonia, Arvo Pärt is one of the pivotal classical composers of the late 20th century. In 1940 Estonia was occupied by the Russians following the Molotov-Ribbentrop Pact, and consequent to the German invasion of Russia in 1941, Estonia, like the rest of Eastern Europe, was to be fought over by the Germans and Russians before the ultimate Soviet triumph in May 1945. For the next forty-five years Estonia was to be firmly part of the Soviet Union, not gaining its independence again until August 1991. Thus, Pärt was to develop musically in an authoritarian regime, largely cut off from mainstream influences from the West.

Above: Men of Estonia's army prepare to resist the 1939 Soviet invasion

Pärt began his musical education at the age of seven and by the end of the 1940s had already started to compose. His education was completed at the Talinn Conservatory, where he studied under Heino Eller. His early works were heavily influenced by composers such as Shostakovich and Prokofiev but he was subsequently to experiment with Arnold Schoenberg's 12-tone technique, a means of ensuring that all twelve notes of the chromatic scale are sounded as often as one another in a piece of music while preventing the emphasis of any through the use of tone row, an ordering of the twelve pitches. All twelve notes are thus given more or less equal importance, and the music avoids being in a key. Pärt's first composition in this style was *Nekrolog*, completed in 1960, which led to official disfavor.

Following this technique he next adopted a "collage" approach in which various styles were utilized; this style too failed to find favor amongst the authorities and, following the completion of his Second Symphony in 1966, Pärt temporarily abandoned composition whilst he undertook a study of medieval choral music from France and the Low Countries. This led to the composition of his first religious piece, *Credo*, in 1968, which was the last of

Above: An Easter service in Moscow's Yelokhovsky Cathedral

"I build with the most primitive materials–with the triad, with one specific tonality. The three notes of a triad are like bells and that is why I call it tintinnabulation."
Pärt, on his regular reference to tintinnabulation–the sound of music of bells–when describing his music

Above: Tallinn, Estonia, where Pärt is now based

his collage pieces but which also offended the secular Soviet Union and was banned despite its popularity. The disfavor that his recent compositions received caused both a breakdown in health and an awareness of the growing role of religion in his life; as a result Pärt became a member of the Russian Orthodox Church.

After a second break from composition, Pärt introduced his "tintinnabulist" period in the mid-1970s, with pieces such as *Für Alina*. Still out of favor with the authorities, he and his second wife–who was Jewish–received permission to emigrate to Israel in 1980. However, they traveled instead to Vienna, where they stayed for eighteen months before settling in Germany, where Pärt continued to compose significant pieces of religious music. One characteristic of Pärt's later works is that they are frequently settings for sacred texts, although he mostly chooses Latin or the Church Slavonic used in Orthodox liturgy instead of his native Estonian.

Following the collapse of the Soviet Union and Estonia's independence in 1991, Pärt returned to his native country at the start of the 21st century and is now based in Talinn. He continues to compose, and completed his Fourth Symphony in 2008.

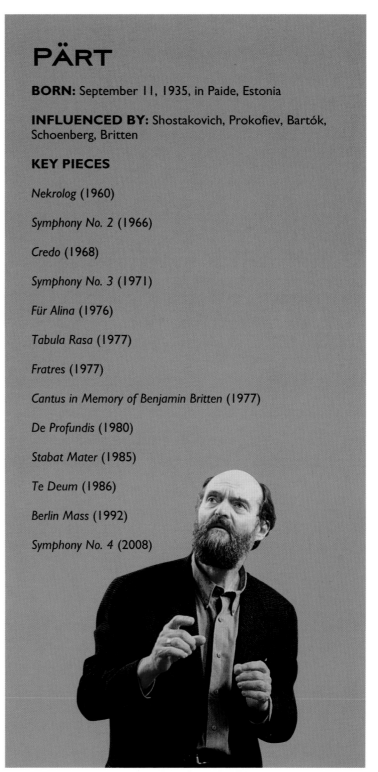

PÄRT

BORN: September 11, 1935, in Paide, Estonia

INFLUENCED BY: Shostakovich, Prokofiev, Bartók, Schoenberg, Britten

KEY PIECES

Nekrolog (1960)

Symphony No. 2 (1966)

Credo (1968)

Symphony No. 3 (1971)

Für Alina (1976)

Tabula Rasa (1977)

Fratres (1977)

Cantus in Memory of Benjamin Britten (1977)

De Profundis (1980)

Stabat Mater (1985)

Te Deum (1986)

Berlin Mass (1992)

Symphony No. 4 (2008)

Other Modern Composers

• **Samuel Barber** *(1910–1981)* The composer Samuel Barber was not prolific in his output, but with his *Adagio for Strings* of 1938 he produced one of the signature pieces of US classical music.

• **Béla Bartók** *(1881–1845)* The Hungarian Bartók was one of the most important composers of the first half of the 20th century. Prolific in composition—he composed no fewer than 436 pieces for the piano—much of his work was rooted in folk music traditions that he researched closely.

Above: Samuel Barber

• **Alban Berg** *(1885–1935)* Heavily influenced by his countryman Schoenberg, Berg developed further his teacher's 12–tone method. Berg was one of the more influential of the Expressionist school of composers, whose work fell out of favor in Germany and Austria as a result of his Jewish faith and the fact that Expressionism was regarded as degenerate art.

• **Leonard Bernstein** *(1918–1990)* Known both for conducting and for composing, the US–born Bernstein was one of the towering figures of late 20th century classical music, whose works have been performed widely on stage and on film. He is perhaps best-known as the composer of *West Side Story*, which was completed in 1957, with lyrics by Stephen Sondheim.

Left: Leonard Bernstein

• **Aaron Copland** *(1900–1990)* Probably the greatest composer to emerge from the USA, Copland's output was, however, relatively limited, numbering some 135 pieces in all. He wrote works that brought together jazz, folk and neo-classical traditions, with his best-known pieces probably being *Fanfare for the Common Man of 1942* and *Appalachian Spring* (1943).

• **George Gershwin** *(1898–1937)* Born of Jewish émigré parents in the USA, Gershwin was heavily influenced by other genres of music, most notably jazz, and composed for the film industry as well as orchestral, chamber and vocal pieces. His most significant works include *Rhapsody in Blue* (1924), *An American in Paris* (1928) and *Porgy and Bess* (1935).

• **Charles Ives** *(1874–1954)* The American composer Charles Ives was one of the pioneers of modernism but paradoxically was also highly conservative, with many of his works owing much to his religious beliefs. Amongst his best-known pieces are *Three Places in New England*, composed between 1903 and 1914, and his *Symphony No. 4* (1916).

Right: Gershwin composing a tune at the piano, c.1935

• **Sergei Prokofiev** *(1891–1953)* A Russian pianist and composer who spent some years in exile before returning to his homeland in 1935, Prokofiev produced seven symphonies, nine operas and ten ballets, as well as film scores and other orchestral pieces.

• **Arnold Schoenberg** *(1874–1951)* One of the most influential composers in the transition from Romantic to Modern classical music, the Austrian-born Schoenberg was a pioneer of developments such as atonality and the 12-tone method.

• **Dmitri Shostakovich** *(1906–1975)* Russian-born, Shostakovich was unusual amongst his fellow Russian composers in that he remained in his homeland throughout the Revolution and the period of Stalin's purges. He was perhaps the most important symphonic composer since Mahler, completing fifteen symphonies in all, along operas, ballets, film scores and other orchestral pieces. His most

Left: Prokofiev, aged 9, at the piano with the score of his opera The Giants

important pieces include the opera *Lady Macbeth of the Mtsensk District* (1936) and his *String Quartet No. 8* (1960), which he composed after having seen the destruction wrought on Dresden fifteen years earlier.

• **Igor Stravinsky** *(1882–1971)* Although not prolific–he composed only 127 worksduring his long life–Stravinsky is regarded as one of the foremost composers of the 20th century. Russian–born, he was, like so many of his compatriots, forced into exile and was ultimately to die in the USA. A noted composer of ballets, his best–known works include *The Rite of Spring* (1913), which was popularized by the Disney film *Fantasia* in 1940, and the opera *The Rake's Progress*, which was premièred in 1951.

• **Sir William Walton** *(1902–1983)* Largely self-taught, the British composer William Walton was ultimately to succeed Elgar as the composer of music for great state occasions and was knighted in 1951. Amongst his most significant classical work was the oratorio *Belshazzar's Feast* of 1931; Walton was also a noted composer of music for films.

Above: Dmitri Shostakovich with the Glazunov Quartet in 1940

Above: Sir William Walton

6 THE ORCHESTRA

Derived from the Greek word for the space in front of the stage in which traditionally the chorus was situated, the word orchestra has come to mean a group of musicians that perform together as an ensemble. The orchestra is normally formed of four sections—brass, percussion, string and woodwind—and its size and actual composition can vary according to the piece of music and the size of hall in which it is being performed. Chamber orchestras normally number about fifty players, whilst the great symphony or philharmonic orchestras can comprise 100 or more.

Each of the four sections of the orchestra has an accepted hierarchy and is led by a principal who can also, when necessary, play the solos, unless they are being performed by a specialist virtuoso. The violins are divided into two groups—first and second—each of which has a principal. The principal within the first violins is normally known as the orchestra's leader and is generally regarded as the conductor's second-in-command, taking responsibility for rehearsal in his absence, and other duties. Each of the other sections also has principals and leaders; the principal oboe, for example, is considered to be the leader of the woodwind section.

The modern orchestra generally includes the following: brass (horns, trumpets, trombones and tuba); percussion (timpani, drums, cymbals, triangles); strings (violins, violas, cellos, double bass); and woodwind (piccolo, flutes, oboes, horn, clarinets, bassoons and contrabassoon). Individual pieces may require the addition of other instruments; piano music, for example, would naturally see the orchestra supplemented by a piano, whilst Saint-Saëns' Organ Symphony requires an organ, thus limiting its performances to concert halls in which one is available.

Although music was played throughout the Middle Ages, the development of the modern orchestra started in the 16th century when composers started to write

Above: Johann Strauss at the Court Ball in Vienna

Right: The Minneapolis Chamber Orchestra

Pages 132–133: La Salle Pleyel concert hall, Paris, one of the few auditoriums specifically built for symphonic music

"Conductors must give unmistakable and suggestive signals to the orchestra–not choreography to the audience."
George Szell

music specifically for musical groups. Much of the stimulus came initially from aristocratic and royal patronage. Many of the early composers were directly or indirectly employed by the nobility to furnish music for the household musicians for entertainment such as dances and masques.

A second stimulus came with the development of the theatre and particularly of opera from the late 16th century onwards. Opera had its origins in Italy, but it was to become influential through much of Western Europe during these formative years. By the end of the 17th century, Italian style opera was popular in England, France and Germany as well as in its home country.

The 18th century saw the modern string family replace the traditional viols, and the rise of the keyboard instrument–initially the harpsichord but later the piano–as the player of the bass-continuo. This latter innovation, however, was to disappear in the 19th century whilst, following Beethoven's influence, the so-called "standard complement" of double winds and brass appeared from the early years of that century. Later in the 19th century the massive works of Richard Wagner brought new demands on the orchestra; his opera *Das Rheingold*, for example, requires no fewer than six harps. The evolution of the orchestra has continued over the years, both in terms of becoming more complex and larger but also, paradoxically, as the fashion grew for recreating historic

music on authentic instruments, smaller and more intimate, reflecting more accurately the scale and sound of the orchestras of the 17th and 18th centuries.

However, the traditional orchestra, its organization, and the instruments that comprise it, have changed significantly over the years. The arrangement of the orchestra has varied with, for example, in the 20th century both the first and second violins seated to the conductor's left, with the cello section to the right. And instruments that have disappeared from the contemporary orchestra, or which have been altered significantly over recent centuries, include:

Strings—lute, viol and the hurdy-gurdy;

Keyboards—harpsichord, virginal, spinet and the clavichord;

Woodwind—shawm, crumhorn and recorder;

Brass—cornett, natural horn and serpent.

Despite the loss of these instruments from the modern orchestra, the revival of interest in playing classical music with original instruments has ensured that the sound that these instruments make is not lost to the contemporary audience.

The next section of the book looks in more detail at the history and development of some of the pivotal instruments of the contemporary orchestra.

Left: An orchestra plays at the Villa Campolieto Ercolano in Naples

THE KEY INSTRUMENTS

"It doesn't matter whether you play the violin, the flute, the cello, or the drums, you're still part of the orchestra."

As outlined in the previous section, the orchestra comprises instruments from a number of families. The string section, for example, includes violins, violas, cellos, double bass, and, when necessary, a harp. There is, however, a number of key instruments that are pivotal to the sound that the orchestra makes and for which musicians have often composed some of the greatest pieces of music within the classical canon. However, these instruments have changed radically over the years and the modern oboe, for example, is very different in complexity and tonal range to that of 17th century France. Although now it is often possible to hear some of the great pieces from the Baroque and Classical periods played on authentic instruments, many of the classic recordings from the mid-20th century onwards played these historic works with the modern versions of the instruments, thus leading to a very different sound to that envisaged by the original composer. This section looks at some of these most influential instruments in greater depth.

Above: Musicans playing the saxophone and the serpent at the Kneller Hall museum of ancient instruments

CELLO

The second largest of the string instruments used in an orchestra, the four-string cello, can be used both as a solo instrument (in pieces such as Elgar's *Cello Concerto*), as part of a string quartet, or as part of the string section of the orchestra. The name is an abbreviated form of the Italian *violoncello* (little violone) and the instrument was developed from the mid-17th century from the bass violin with the development in northern Italy of the wire-wound strings (fine wire around a thin gut core) that permitted a finer bass sound. Modern cellos differ from earlier instruments in several ways. Modern cellos, for example, have an endpin at the bottom to support the instrument (and transmit some of the sound through the floor), while Baroque cellos are held only by the calves of the player.

Modern strings normally have a metal core, although some use a synthetic core; Baroque strings are made of gut, with the G and C strings wire-wound. Overall, the modern instrument has much higher string tension than the Baroque cello, resulting in a louder, more projecting tone with fewer overtones. The modern symphony orchestra normally includes between eight and twelve cellists, who sit on the right-hand side of the orchestra (as viewed by the audience) opposite the violin players. There have been a number of notable musicians and composers who have been initially cellists; these include Pablo Casals, Jacqueline de Pré, Jacques Offenbach and Arturo Toscanini.

Above: British cellist Jacqueline Du Pre performing with pianist and conductor Daniel Barenboim

CLARINET

"At the beginning of the current [18th] century, he invented a new kind of pipe-work, the so-called clarinet... and at length presented an improved chalumeau."

Johann Gabriel Doppelmeyr in 1730 on Denner's alleged role in developing the clarinet

One of the single-reed instruments that form part of the woodwind section of the orchestra, the name clarinet is derived from the Italian suffix *et* (meaning little) and *clarion* (referring to a type of trumpet). The clarinet has a cylindrical bore and its pitch is varied by the pitch holes in the tube. The fingering of the instrument is particularly complicated. The clarinet is believed to have been invented by Johann Christoph Denner at the start of the 18th century, although the physical evidence for this is suspect.

The clarinet differed from the earlier chalumeau by the addition of a register key. More keys and airtight pads were subsequently added to improve tone. The clarinet represents a family of instruments of differing sizes and

Above: Three girls play clarinets in a marching band in Trondheim, Norway

pitches; the most common, however, is the B ♭ soprano clarinet. The classical orchestra normally includes two clarinetists, although from the late 19th century, pieces requiring three or more were composed. The clarinet can also be used as a solo instrument; composers such as Mozart composed concertos for the instrument and it is particularly popular in chamber music.

DRUMS

The drum is a member of the percussion group of musical instruments and is technically classified as membranous. Historically, the drum represents the world's oldest and most ubiquitous instrument, with a wide range of uses. In the orchestra the most common drums in use are the kettledrum, the bass drum, the side drum and the tenor drum. Kettledrums—or timpani—are unusual amongst drums, being capable of producing an actual pitch when struck and can be tuned with the use of a pedal mechanism to control each drum's range of notes. Developed from military drums, the kettledrum had become central to the orchestra by the end of the 18th century. The standard set of kettledrums is four, although pieces of music have been written for more; *The Rite of Spring* by Stravinsky, for example, uses five.

Although the first pieces scored for timpani date from the late 17th century—with Jean-Baptiste Lully's 1695 opera *Thésée* being the first—it was during the late 18th century with Beethoven that their role was revolutionized. The orchestral bass drum is the largest drum in the orchestra and was developed from the davul, an instrument imported from the Middle East. The side, or snare, drum arose from the medieval tabor drum that was improved in the 17th century onwards. A tenor drum is a cylindrical drum that is higher pitched than a bass drum and similar in size to a field snare, but without snares and played with soft mallets or hard sticks.

Under various names, the drum has been used by composers since the mid-19th century, and it is particularly noticeable in scores by twentieth-century English composers such as Britten and Walton, and American composers such as Copland.

In the orchestra, the percussion section is situated at the back, directly in front of the conductor, with the drums located to the conductor's left.

Left: The drum section of the National Ballet of China Symphony Orchestra

Right: The London Symphonic Orchestra Shell Scholarship Percussion Final Concert, July 1992

FLUTE

One of the key instruments within the woodwind section, the flute–originally constructed in wood but today generally made from metal, and with keywork that largely dates from the 19th century–is the descendant of one of the oldest and most basic of instruments. Unlike other woodwind instruments that require a reed to play, the flute is reedless, with the player blowing over a hole–known as the embouchure–with the range of notes being produced by a sequence of holes. Originally the holes were covered and opened as required by fingers, but they were later replaced by the metal keywork. Related to the flute, but smaller, is the piccolo. The earliest identifiable flute-type instruments date back almost 40,000 years to central Europe.

The earliest extant example of a flute is a lacquered bamboo instrument from China that has been dated to the mid-5th century BC. The transverse flute reached Europe from the Far East, via the Byzantine Empire, during the Medieval period. Used in court and secular music, particularly in France and Germany, its use became more widespread as it was adopted for military purposes in the late 15th century. As with the trumpet, the flute was to be used widely for the purposes of signaling. Its popularity grew during the 16th and 17th centuries when the flute was widely used in the scores of ballet, chamber and opera music, and composers such as Telemann and Vivaldi wrote music specifically for the instrument.

With the development of the symphony orchestra from the 18th century, the position of the flute became central, although it was to fall out of favor during the 19th century before being rediscovered later in that century through composers such as Debussy. Much of the success of the flute from the mid-19th century was the result of the German Thomas Böhm who patented his model of flute in 1847. Böhm's key system is still regarded as the basis of the modern instrument.

As part of the woodwind section, the flautists sit directly in front of the conductor but to his left and directly in front of the clarinets.

Left: James Galway playing his flute

FRENCH HORN

The French horn–as the horn is known in the Anglophonic world–is one of the instruments that form the brass section of the orchestra. Effectively an elongated tube of metal of some twelve feet in length, but coiled, the variations in pitch that the horn produces are made by valves. Prior to the development of the valves in the first half of the 19th century, the horn was a much more basic instrument, with changes of pitch being achieved by the use of the lips alone. The horn was historically used widely in the hunt, as the sound it made could carry over a wide distance. As a result of this, horns were often used in early classical music to suggest the hunt. From the mid-18th century the range of the horn was extended by the technique called hand-stopping, pioneered by the Czech, Anton Joseph Hampel, and widely adopted by the Bohemian Jan Václav Stich (who was better known as Giovanni Punto, the name he adopted in Italy).

This technique, that involved inserting a cupped hand into the bell of the natural horn, allowed the player to reduce the pitch of a note by more than a semitone and permitted the horn to become an instrument capable, even without valves, of more melodic work. Thus, from the mid-18th century, music

"Who is this Beethoven? His name is not known to us. Of course, Punto is very well known."
A critic writing in 1800 about the noted payer of the French Horn, Giovanni Punto

specifically designed to capitalize upon the increased capability of the horn was composed. Mozart, for example, composed four concerti for horns, whilst an earlier generation–including Mozart's father Leopold, Telemann, Bach and Handel–all used the horn to create specific effects. Once the horn with valves was developed, composers further exploited its capabilities with works such as Richard Strauss's *Till Eulenspiegels lustige Streiche (Till Eulenspiegel's Merry Pranks*; Till Eulenspiegel being a German peasant folk hero) making full use of the chromatic range that the modified instrument now offered. The horn section of the orchestra is generally sited left of centre, sandwiched between the clarinets in front and the harp (if required) behind.

KEYBOARDS

"[Handel] had found means to get a little clavichord privately convey'd to a room at the top of the house. To this room he constantly stole when the family was asleep. He had made some progress before Music had been prohibited, and by his assiduous practice at hours of rest, had made such farther advances, as, tho' not attended to at that time, were no slight prognostications of his future greatness."

John Mainwaring, Memoirs of the Life of the late G. F. Handel, *referring to the unwillingness of Handel's father to permit his musical son's education*

Developed from the harpsichord in the late 17th or early 18th century by the Italian Bartolomeo Cristofero, the piano is now one of the most familiar and popular instruments to be used in classical music, with a wide range of pieces composed specifically for it. It can be used for solo performance or in conjunction with a chamber or symphony orchestra. Being an ideal instrument for practice and composition, many of the greatest classical composers were noted pianists, including Beethoven, Chopin, Debussy, Liszt, Mendelssohn, Mozart, Prokofiev and Schumann. When a piano is required for orchestral concerts, it is generally sited directly in front of the conductor.

The first attempts to create keyboard instruments occurred during the middle ages with instruments such as the hurdy-gurdy. Prior to the invention of the piano, the most common form of keyboard instrument in classical music was the harpsichord. Unlike the piano, where the strings are struck, in the harpsichord family—which includes the virginal, the muselar

Left: An ornate harpsichord decorated in blue, red and gold

and the spinet—the strings are plucked. The harpsichord was invented in the late medieval period and was widely used in Renaissance and Baroque music, and although pieces continued to be composed for it through to the 19th century, it was largely superseded by the piano from the early 18th century. However, the harpsichord has re-emerged in the 20th century, as the fashion to play mediaeval and Baroque music on authentic instruments has developed.

Another keyboard instrument to predate the piano was the clavichord, although this was rarely used in performance, as it failed to produce a note loud enough to be heard by a large audience, but was widely used for practice and composition. Unlike the harpsichord, the strings of the clavichord were struck and so was a true precursor of the piano.

Apart from the piano, occasionally the organ is also used, say for pieces such as Camille Saint-Saëns' Symphony No. 3. Performance of these pieces obviously require the presence of an organ and so are limited to the larger concert halls, such as, in London, the Royal Festival Hall and the Royal Albert Hall.

OBOE

A double-reed instrument that forms part of the woodwind section of the orchestra, the name oboe—which became popular in English after c1770 as replacement to a variety of earlier names such as the "French hoboy"—was derived from the Italian word *oboè*, which itself was derived from two French words *haut* (high or loud) and *bois* (wood). It was developed from the mid-17th century in France, where it was known originally as the *hautbois*, as a progression from the earlier Shawm. There were a number of differences between the Shawm and the Baroque oboe; these included the division of the latter into three parts, which improved the quality of its manufacture, and the development of the wind-cap, which was placed over the reed and which allowed for the production of a louder volume. The Baroque oboe had three keys—a great key and two side keys—that provided a wider range of notes than that possible with the earlier instruments.

The next phase of the development of the oboe occurred in the 18th century when the conical boring of the instrument was narrowed and additional keys were added. As the range of the instrument grew, so composers increasingly wrote pieces specifically for it. A number of chamber and symphonic pieces that include solo parts for the oboe were composed by, for example, Mozart, Haydn and Beethoven. The oboe was further developed during the 19th century by the Triebert family in Paris; this work added to the range of keys available and the instrument has undergone further modification since then.

The woodwind section of the orchestra is located in the centre of the orchestra, situated between the brass section and the conductor. The oboes are seated to the right of the conductor

Right: French oboist, composer, and conductor Maurice Bourgue

TRUMPET

"Notwithstanding the real loftiness and distinguished nature of its quality of tone, there are few instruments that have been more degraded [than the trumpet]. Down to Beethoven and Weber, every composer–not excepting Mozart–persisted in confining it to the unworthy function of filling up, or in causing it to sound two or three commonplace rhythmical formulae."

Hector Berlioz, on the natural trumpet in 1844

A member of the brass family of instruments, the trumpet has the highest register of the brass section and can claim to be one of the oldest instruments in origin, dating back more than 3,500 years. The earliest trumpets were largely used for military purposes, a function that is replicated today by the bugle, for the dissemination of instructions. The original–or natural–trumpet consisted of a single coiled tube without valves, which could therefore only produce notes of a single overtone series. During the 16th and 17th centuries trumpets with differing bores and mouthpieces were used in groups to produce different portions of the harmonic range. The Baroque period is widely regarded as the golden age of the natural trumpet, with pieces such as Jeremiah Clarke's *Prince of Denmark's March*–better known as the *Trumpet Voluntary*–being one of the familiar works from that period.

The trumpet fell out of favor during the late 18th century as a result of its lack of range, although composers such as Mozart, Beethoven and Brahms all composed music that required the use of natural trumpets. From the 18th century there were attempts to develop a keyed trumpet, but these were, however, initially unsuccessful until, in 1818, Friedrich Bluhmel and Heinrich Stötzel made a patent application for the box valve. One of the first pieces of music specifically composed for the chromatic–as opposed to natural–trumpet was Haydn's *Trumpet Concerto* (1796). Once the trumpet was capable of achieving a greater range of notes, so its importance to the orchestra grew. More recently, however, with the trend towards playing historic music on authentic instruments, the natural trumpet has made a comeback and can be heard regularly in pieces for which it was originally intended.

The trumpet section of the orchestra normally sits in the centre, directly in front of the drum section.

TUBA

The largest and lowest-pitched of the brass instruments, the tuba is a relatively recent addition to the orchestra, having originally been patented by Wilhelm Friedrich Wieprecht and Carl Moritz in September 1835, replacing the ophicleide (itself an earlier nineteenth-century invention that had supplanted the serpent. Brass instruments generally are either bored conically or cylindrically; the tuba family—that includes the euphonium, the sousaphone and the bombardon—have wide conical bores. The tuba and trombone section of the orchestra is normally situated towards the center, directly in front of the conductor, towards the rear. An orchestra will generally have a single tuba player, although there are pieces for which a second is sometimes required. There are a number of well-known classical pieces—such as Stravinsky's *Rite of Spring* and Richard Strauss's *Also sprach Zarathustra* and *Eine Alpensinfonie*—that include significant parts for the tuba.

"The tuba is certainly the most intestinal of instruments, the very lower bowel of music."
Peter De Vries

Right: A tuba player in the Lofthouse and Middlehouse Silver Band

VIOLIN

Originally the name of a family of instruments rather than a single instrument, the violin, which is normally fitted with four strings, developed its distinct form from the mid-16th century. A member of the string section of the orchestra, the violin is related to the viola, cello and double-bass. It was, however at the end of the 17th and early 18th centuries, with the work of Antonio Stradivari, that the violin became perfected, and it was no coincidence that the instrument became one of the most important within the orchestra from the Baroque era onwards. From the late 18th century, the position of the violin was further enhanced when the string quartet became the norm for chamber music.

The tone of the violin is superior to many other instruments, and this makes it appropriate for playing the melodic line, given that it is capable of rapid and difficult sequences of notes. Violins form a large part of the orchestra and are usually divided into two sections—first and second violins—with the first section led by principal violinist, who is normally also the leader of the orchestra. The principal violinist often handles rehearsals in the absence of the conductor.

With the ability of the violin to play complex pieces of music, many pieces have been composed featuring it as a solo instrument; composers such as Mendelssohn, Bruch, Brahms, Mozart and Beethoven have all written violin concerti. Over the years, some of the most prominent and well-known classical musicians have also been violinists, including Johann Sebastian Bach, Joseph Haydn, Mozart, Niccolò Paganini and Yehudi Menuhin.

Above: Violinist and conductor Yehudi Menuhin

7 Great Symphony Orchestras

Across the globe there are countless symphony orchestras, with most major cities possessing at least one, and many broadcasters, such as the BBC, also controlling one or more. There is, however, a number of orchestras that have a worldwide reputation as a result of their history, their association with the great conductors and their repertoire. The following section looks at a number of these orchestras and their history.

"I don't feel that the conductor has real power. The orchestra has the power, and every member of it knows instantaneously if you're just beating time."
Itzhak Perlman

Below: Daniel Harding conducting the Deutsche Kammerphilharmonie Bremen Orchestra at The Barbican in London

BERLIN PHILHARMONIC

Called originally *Frühere Bilsesche Kapelle* (Former Bilse's Band) when established in 1882 by fifty-four musicians, Die Berliner Philharmoniker adopted its current name in 1887. Widely regarded as one of the best symphony orchestras in the world–it was voted as number two in the world by *Gramophone* magazine in 2008–its reputation was initially established from the start by the appointment of one of the world's then leading conductors, Hans von Bülow, as its conductor. The reputation that the orchestra soon earned encouraged many of the leading composers of the age–such as Brahms, Grieg and Mahler–to conduct it. The orchestra has, over the years, been led by some of the greatest conductors, including Wilhelm Furtwängler (from 1923 until 1945), Herbert von Karajan (1955 until 1989), and Claudio Abbado (1989 until 2002). Since 2002 the orchestra has been led by the British conductor Sir Simon Rattle, who made his name initially at the City of Birmingham Symphony Orchestra. Since Karajan's departure in 1989, the orchestra's range has expanded from the core classical and romantic music, often German in origin, with which the orchestra had been traditionally associated, into including more twentieth-century work in its repertoire.

Left: The Chamber Music Hall of the Berlin Philharmonic, built in 1987 by Edgar Wisniewski

Boston Symphony Orchestra

One of the "Big Five" of US orchestras—the others are the Chicago Symphony Orchestra, the Cleveland Orchestra, the New York Philharmonic and the Philadelphia Orchestra—the Boston Symphony Orchestra, based at the city's Symphony Hall (a classical concert hall opened in 1900), was founded in 1881 by Henry Lee Higginson. From 1924 until 1949 the orchestra was under the musical direction of the Russian, Serge Koussevitzky, and it was during these years that the orchestra's reputation started to grow. It was under Koussevitzky that notable works by composers such as Prokofiev and Stravinsky were commissioned and given their premières.

The orchestra made its first recording in 1917 and its first stereo recording in 1954. Working with both the orchestra's musical directors and with notable guest conductors, the orchestra has recorded a significant number of works and has also been involved in providing the music for a number of notable films, such as *Schindler's List* and *Saving Private Ryan*. The current musical director is James Levine who, on his appointment in 2004, became the first US-born conductor to hold the position.

Above: The original Boston Symphony Orchestra on stage, 1882

LONDON SYMPHONY ORCHESTRA

Based at the Barbican Centre in London since 1982, the London Symphony Orchestra was founded in 1904 and was the first such orchestra to be established in the United Kingdom. The first principal conductor was the Austrian, Hans Richter, who was succeeded for a year by Edward Elgar in 1911. Another early conductor was Thomas Beecham, who was in charge for a brief period during World War I. More recent principal conductors have included André Previn (1968-1979), Claudio Abbado (1979-1988), Michael Tilson Thomas (1988-1995) and Sir Colin Davis (1995-2006). The current [2010] principal conductor is the Russian Valery Gergiev. The LSO was the first British orchestra to play overseas when, in 1906, it traveled to Paris, and was also the first British orchestra to play at the Salzburg Festival when invited there in 1973. In April 1912 the orchestra was booked to travel on the ill-fated liner *Titanic* on the ship's maiden voyage; fortunately, it had to alter its travel arrangements before the ship sailed. The LSO has made numerous recordings over the years–indeed it now has its own record label (LSO Live)–and commissioned pieces from many of the leading twentieth-century composers. The orchestra is also well known for its involvement in the film industry, providing the music for a number of classic movies, including *Star Wars, Raiders of the Lost Ark, Superman* and *Braveheart*.

Right: Russian conductor Valery Gergiev with the London Symphony Orchestra at The Barbican in London

ROYAL CONCERTGEBOUW ORCHESTRA

Established originally in 1888, the Koninklijk Concertgebouworkest is based in Amsterdam. Originally known only as the Concertgebouworkest, it became "Royal" in 1988 when granted the title by Queen Beatrix to mark the orchestra's centenary. In 2008 *Gramophone* magazine named the Concertgebouworkest as the world's top symphony orchestra. The orchestra is based in the Concertgebouw, a stunning classical building opened originally in April 1888 shortly before the foundation of the orchestra; this, with the Musikverein in Vienna and the Symphony Hall in Boston, are regarded as the three greatest concert halls in the world.

Between 1895 and 1988 the orchestra was effectively dominated by three great leaders: Willem Mengelberg (from 1895 to 1945); Eduard van Beinum (1945 to 1959); and, Bernard Haitink (1961 to 1988). Under Megelberg, the orchestra was known for championing the then contemporary composers such Mahler and Richard Strauss. Van Beinum was a specialist in the works of Anton Bruckner and his recordings of this Austrian composer were important in helping to establish Bruckner's posthumous reputation. Under Haitink, the Concertgebouworkest became one of the leading orchestras for recording music, with contracts with companies such as the Dutch-based Philips and the British company EMI. The orchestra is currently [2010] led by the Latvian conductor Mariss Jansons.

Above: Mariss Jansons conducting the Royal Concertgebouw Orchestra at The Barbican, London

Right: The Concertgebouw Concert Hall in Amsterdam

VIENNA PHILHARMONIC

First formed in 1842, the Wiener Philharmoniker was founded by Otto Nicolai as the Philharmonische Academie and is today regarded as one of the best symphony orchestras in Europe. The Philharmonische Academie was a fully independent orchestra that took all its decisions by a democratic vote of all its members, a principle the orchestra still holds today. In 1860 the new conductor, Karl Anton Eckert, launched a series of four subscription concerts, a marking point from which the orchestra has performed continuously. Until 1933, the orchestra, like others, employed a principal conductor; these included, between 1898 and 1901, the composer Gustav Mahler. Since 1933, however, the orchestra has used primarily guest conductors, and many of the greatest names in classical music have conducted the orchestra at various times. These have included Richard Strauss, Karl Böhm, Leonard Bernstein, Herbert von Karajan and Daniel Barenboim. The orchestra is based at the Musikverein (Music Association), which is a classical concert hall opened originally in 1870; this is considered to be one of the three finest concert halls in the world. The orchestra runs a number of subscription concerts, for which the waiting list for tickets can stretch for years.

Left: The rust and white facade of the Musikverein building in Vienna

Pages 166–167: The Vienna Symphony Orchestra and the Vienna Philharmonic String Quartet perform at the ceremonial opening of Vienna's Theater an der Wien in 1962

8 MAJOR CONDUCTORS

Although the composer is rightly credited with the actual composition of the piece of movement, much of the resulting sound can be attributed to the skills of, and interpretation by, the conductor. Although most conductors will be able to conduct orchestras in any piece of music, many have over the years become associated particularly with the works of one or two composers. The dynamic relationship between the orchestra and the conductor can often lead to strains and stresses, with the result that many of the best-known conductors have often proved to be slightly larger than life characters.

"To Strauss the composer I take off my hat; to Strauss the man I put it back on again."
Toscanini, referring to Richard Strauss's involvement with the Third Reich

Left: Italian conductor Arturo Toscanini leads the NBC Symphony Orchestra at a concert in 1949

SIR THOMAS BEECHAM

Born on April 28, 1879, in St Helens, Lancashire, into a wealthy manufacturing family (his grandfather had founded the Beecham's Pills business), Beecham was educated at Rossall School. Forbidden by his father to attend a music conservatoire in Germany, he went up to Wadham College, Oxford, but left in 1898 after only a year. Studying music privately in London, Beecham was largely self-taught as a conductor. He first conducted publicly in October 1899 and again the following month when he replaced Hans Richter as conductor of the Hallé Orchestra at a concert held to mark his father's inauguration as Mayor of St Helens.

Beecham's professional debut occurred three years later in London. In 1906 he founded what was to become the New Symphony Orchestra, conducting many recently composed pieces rather than more familiar and popular works. He left the NSO after two years and was to found the Beecham Symphony Orchestra in 1909; this was also the year that his 10-year estrangement from his father ended and he was able to draw upon the family wealth to subsidize his musical activities, including staging operas at Covent Garden. Again, these tended to be more avant garde than those staged by other impresarios.

Above: Sir Thomas Beecham: portrait by Emu, 1917

During the 1920s Beecham worked closely with the London Symphony Orchestra, but following disagreements he went on to found the London Philharmonic Orchestra with Malcolm Sargent. The new orchestra made its debut to critical acclaim in October 1932, and during the 1930s the LPO made more than 300 recordings and appeared in numerous concerts. In 1936 the orchestra undertook a controversial tour of Germany, where Adolf Hitler attended one of the concerts.

Between 1941 and 1944 Beecham was based in Australia and then North America, where, from 1942, he was the joint senior conductor of the Metropolitan Opera in New York. Returning to London, Beecham rejoined the London Philharmonic but in his absence the orchestra had become a self-governing co-operative and, although the concerts held under his baton proved hugely successful, the relationship was broken and Beecham left to found, in 1946, the Royal Philharmonic Orchestra. Apart from work with the RPO, Beecham also conducted at Glyndebourne during the late 1940s.

Beecham was to be associated with the RPO for the remainder of his life, taking the orchestra on several overseas tours and also undertaking an exhaustive program of concerts in London. Apart from his work with the RPO, both live and in the recording studio, Beecham continued to conduct opera in Britain and abroad. He was a noted conductor of the works of the Bradford-born composer Frederick Delius and also of Richard Strauss, doing much to popularize both composers through concerts and recordings.

Beecham died on March 8, 1961, having conducted for the last time, in Portsmouth, on May 7, 1960.

BERNARD HAITINK

"Every conductor, including myself, has a sell-by date."
Bernard Haitink in 2006, declining the role of Music Director to the Chicago Symphony Orchestra

Born on March 4, 1929, in Amsterdam, Bernard Johan Herman Haitink is a Dutch conductor who was one of the handful of conductors of the Concertgebouworkest that established it as one of the world's greatest. Originally trained as a violinist at the Conservatoire in Amsterdam, he subsequently took courses in conducting in 1954 and 1955. His first professional position was as second conductor of the Netherlands Radio Union Orchestra in 1955, and he made his debut with the Concertgebouw in November 1956, replacing the scheduled conductor, Carlo Maria Giulini. In September 1959 he became the first conductor of the Concertgeboow, being promoted to Principal Conductor alongside Eugen Jochum in 1961. He became sole Principal Conductor two years later.

Haitink was to remain as Principal Conductor until 1988. During these years he was also Principal Conductor of the London Philharmonic Orchestra (1967-79) and music director of Glyndebourne Opera (1978-1988). From 1987 until 2002 Haitink was Music Director of the Royal Opera House in London, and from 2002 until 2004 was chief conductor of the Dresden Staatskapelle; he resigned from the latter position two years before his contract was due to end, as a result of disagreements over his possible successor. As a conductor, Haitink has produced recordings of a wide range of composers from the 19th and 20th centuries, including a recent series with the London Symphony Orchestra of all the Beethoven and Brahms symphonies.

Above: Bernard Haitink during a rehearsal for the Glyndebourne Festival Opera's production of Capriccio *in 1987*

Herbert Von Karajan

"Probably the world's best-known conductor and one of the most powerful figures in classical music."
New York Times *obituary, 1989*

Herbert Ritter von Karajan was born in Salzburg, Austria, on April 5, 1908. A child prodigy on the piano, he studied at the Mozarteum–the University of Music and Dramatic Arts–in Salzburg from 1916 until 1926. Whilst there he was encouraged to train as a conductor. His first musical appointment was as Kapellmeister at the Stadttheater in Ulm, Germany, a post that he held from 1929 until 1934. In 1933 he conducted at the Salzburg Festival for the first time and also joined the Nazi Party; the latter was to be a source of much criticism in his later career. In 1934 he conducted the Vienna Philharmonic for the first time and was to be a regular guest conductor for that orchestra thereafter.

In 1935 von Karajan became Germany's youngest Generalmusikdirektor before conducting the Berlin Philharmonic and the Berlin State Opera for the first time two years later. In the late 1930s he became known as a major conductor of the works of Richard Wagner, works that were much in favor amongst the Nazi leadership of the time, and in 1938 signed a recording contract with Deutsche Grammophon.

During his life, von Karajan was to become the world's top-selling artist of classical music; later he was to be one of the leading proponents of the CD and, in 1980, conducted the first-ever recording to be released commercially on CD (a version of Richard Strauss's *Eine Alpensinfonie*).

As a result of his Nazi connections, von Karajan was forced to undergo a "de-Nazification" process post-war and, for the period when Austria was under Allied (including Russian)

occupation, he was banned from conducting in his native land until 1947. However, his career continued to develop, and he became artistic director of the Gesellschaft der Musikfreunde in Wien (Society of Music Friends in Vienna) in 1949 and also conducted at La Scala, with the Philharmonia Orchestra in London, and at the Bayreuth Festival.

In 1955 he became music director of the Berlin Philharmonic, an orchestra with which he was to be closely associated for the rest of his life, whilst also acting as artistic director of the Vienna State Opera (1957-64) and working with both the Vienna Philharmonic and the Salzburg Festival. As a conductor, he had a particular affinity with the major composers from the 19th and early 20th centuries, including Mahler, Sibelius and Nielsen. Von Karajan resigned from his position with the Berlin Philharmonic a few months before his death on July 16, 1989.

Sir Simon Rattle

"Probably the best new version of the Requiem I've heard in quite some years."
Review in BBC Music Magazine *of Rattle's 2007 recording of Brahms's* Ein deutsches Requiem

Born on January 19, 1955, in Liverpool, England, Simon Rattle entered the Royal Academy of Music in London in 1971. In 1974, the year of his graduation in which he won the John Player Conductor Competition, he was appointed assistant conductor of the Bournemouth Symphony Orchestra. Three years later he took on the same role with the Royal Liverpool Philharmonic before moving, in 1980, to become the principal conductor and artistic adviser to the City of Birmingham Symphony Orchestra. In 1990 he became the CBSO's Music Director, and four years later he was knighted, "for services to music". Under his control, the CBSO's profile was enhanced considerably, aided by a move to the city's new Symphony Hall in 1999. A noted conductor of composers of the late 19th and early 20th centuries, and of Mahler in particular, it was with that composer's 6th Symphony that Rattle first conducted the Berlin Philharmonic in 1987.

In 2002 Rattle succeeded Claudio Abbado as the Berlin Philharmonic's Principal Conductor, a role that he is still fulfilling in 2010. Although not universally praised by the critics and with a relationship that he himself describes as "turbulent … [but] never destructively so" with the orchestra, Rattle's contract to run the orchestra has been extended until 2018. Under Rattle's control, the orchestra has been reorganized as a more independent foundation.

Right: The City of Birmingham Symphony Orchestra Hall, where Rattle established his reputation

ARTURO TOSCANINI

"The greatest conductor in the world."
Mussolini on Toscanini

Widely regarded as one of the greatest conductors of the 20th century and one of the pioneers of musical recording and broadcasting, Arturo Toscanini was born on March 25, 1867, in Parma, Italy. Studying the cello at the local conservatoire, he joined an orchestra linked to an opera company on a tour of South America in 1886. During the tour, the company's established conductors failed to succeed and the 19-year-old, with his almost photographic memory of scores, was persuaded to step into the breach. With no formal training, he succeeded with aplomb and the tour helped to establish him on the path to a career as a conductor.

Returning to Italy he initially continued to play the cello as well while simultaneously starting to foster a career as a conductor. In 1896 he conducted his first symphonic concert and became the resident conductor the La Scala opera house, Milan, two years later. He held the role until 1908, and as his reputation grew, so Toscanini's world expanded: he worked with the New York Metropolitan Opera (1908-1915), with the New York Philharmonic Orchestra (1926-36) and was the first non-German to conduct the Wagner festival at Bayreuth (1931-32). His first recordings were made in the early 1920s whilst touring the USA with the La Scala Orchestra.

Although he initially flirted with Fascism, he became an ardent opponent of Benito

Right: Arturo Toscanini conducting at La Scala, Milan, in 1946

Mussolini from the early 1920s onwards and was forced into exile in the 1930s until 1946. In 1937, now based in the USA, Toscanini took charge of the newly-created NBC Symphony Orchestra, with his first broadcast concert being made in December of that year. The next year he conducted the world première of one of the most haunting pieces of American music–Samuel Barber's *Adagio for Strings*. Apart for three years, from 1941 until 1944, Toscanini was to be associated with the NBCSO until his death. Many of his broadcasts were recorded and have been subsequently released. Toscanini died in New York on January 16, 1957. As a conductor, Toscanini was particularly noted for his work with Beethoven, Brahms, Debussy, Richard Strauss and Wagner, as well as Italian composers such as Puccini, Rossini and Verdi.

THE MUSIC ON THE CD

1. **Anon** *Benedicamus Domino, alleluia*
(ad dimittendum populum)
Gregorian chant, named after Gregory I, the Pope from 590 to 604, who is traditionally regarded as having simplified church music and linked it much more to specific services and ceremonies. During the Middle Ages, although Gregorian chant was predominant, it was not the only form of monophonic liturgical music to exist within the Catholic Church. Gregorian chant falls into two main groups: Music of the Mass and Music of the Hours. Gregorian chant was sung virtually unchanged through until the Reformation but was effectively replaced and the tradition lost during the 16th century. It was rediscovered in the early 20th century by the Benedictine monastery at Solesmes in France, and has become increasingly popular since then.

2. **Tallis** *Spem in Alium*
Thomas Tallis was one the pre-eminent composers of the 16th century and one who faced the problem of reconciling composition with the ever-changing religious background. Although the actual date of the composition of *Spem in Alium* is uncertain, it is generally regarded as having been composed around 1570, and such is the scale of the piece that it may have been designed for a special occasion—such as the 40th birthday of Queen Elizabeth in 1573. The original Latin text for the piece is derived from the Book of Judith. The piece is a remarkable achievement in both content and form in that it was written for the extraordinarily large number of forty voices—being split into eight choirs of five voices each—and is rightly regarded as one of the greatest pieces of Renaissance polyphony.

3. **Pachelbel** *Canon in D*
Johann Pachelbel (1653–1706) was a noted German composer of the Baroque period who is now best-known for his *Canon in D*. The piece was written in c1680 and is often played in conjunction with the accompanying *Gigue*. In the piece three violins play the canon, playing the same music but entering two bars apart, whilst a basso continuo, forming the harmonic structure of the piece—a simple eight-note harmony that is repeated more than fifty times. Like many Baroque pieces the *Canon and Fuge in D* remained largely unknown until first published in 1919 but its popularity has increased significantly over the past half-century and is now one of the most widely played pieces from the era, regularly featuring alongside Vivaldi's *Four Seasons* and Albinoni's *Adagio*.

4. **Purcell** *Dido and Aeneas* (Z626) Dido's Lament "When I Am Laid in Earth"
Henry Purcell was England's foremost composer of the late 17th century and, during his relatively short life, was to be hugely prolific, producing a vast quantity of both sacred and secular music. The three-act opera *Dido and Aeneas*, based on the story outlined in Book IV Virgil's *Aeneid* of the doomed love affair between Aeneas and Dido, Queen of Carthage, during Aeneas's journey from Troy via Carthage to Italy, was first performed in early 1689. The libretto was written by Nahum Tate (1652–1715) and the completed work was Purcell's first (and only) fully sung opera. It represents one of the greatest of all Baroque operas and is probably Purcell's most important works for the theater. The lament featured here comes towards the end of the third and final act and is the last aria to be sung by Dido before her death.

5. **Bach** *Chorale movement No 10 Jesus bleibet meine Freude from Herz und Mund und Tat und Leben (Heart and Mouth and Deed and Life)*
Better known to contemporary audiences as *Jesu Joy of Man's Desiring*, this section from one of Johann Sebastian Bach's most important cantatas (BWV147) was written when the composer was in Leipzig for the Christian festival of the Visitation of the Blessed Virgin Mary and was first

performed on July 2, 1723. The music of this section was inspired by the work of an earlier German composer (Johann Schop c1590–1667). Bach scored the chorale movements for choir, trumpet, violin, optionally oboe, viola and basso continuo. The music's wide popularity has led to numerous arrangements and transcriptions, the best-known being that for piano by Dame Myra Hess.

6. **Vivaldi** *The Four Seasons* Opus 8 (RV297): No 4 in F Minor *L'Inverno (Winter)* 2nd Movement (Largo)
Undoubtedly one of the best-known pieces of the Baroque repertoire, *The Four Seasons*, composed by Antonio Vivaldi, was first published in 1725 in Amsterdam. The four concertos for violin and orchestra were part of a set of twelve known as Il cimento dell-armonia e dell'inventione *(The Trial of Strength Between Harmony and Invention)*. The first of the quartet, *Spring*, tells of the goatherd asleep with his faithful dog alongside him. The next, *Summer*, records the heat as the sun beats down on the farm before the weather breaks and a violent hailstorm results. The third part, *Autumn*, covers the harvest and the hunt. The fourth and final part, *Winter*, paints a vivid picture of shivering cold, biting wind and snow alongside the pleasures of the hearth. The piece featured here, the 2nd Movement of *L'Inverna*, is perhaps one of the most beautiful parts of the concerto in which the solo violin sings over a pizzicato background just as heat tries to counter the bitter cold.

7. **Handel** *Hallelujah Chorus* (from *Messiah*)
George Frederic Handel was the founding father of the British tradition of oratorio composition, and in *Messiah*, first performed in Dublin in 1742, he created one of the undoubtedly most popular and instantly recognizable pieces of classical music. The full oratorio lasts for about two hours and provides an interpretation of the prophecies of Christ, his birth, miracles, crucifixion, resurrection and ascension before his ultimate triumph over death itself. The libretto for the oratorio was written by Charles Jennens and was largely based on the translation of the Bible into English and published in the King James and Great Bible versions. The source text for the *Hallelujah Chorus* was Isaiah IX: 6 "For unto us a child is born, unto us a Son is given, and the government shall be upon His shoulder, and

his name shall be called: Wonderful. Counsellor, The Mighty God, The Everlasting Father, The Prince of Peace!"

8. **Mozart** *Overture* to *Die Zauberflöte (The Magic Flute)*
Composed towards the end of Mozart's life and premièred in 1791 shortly before his death, *The Magic Flute* (K620) was an opera in two acts with a libretto by Wolfgang Schikaneder. The opera is in the form of a Singspiel, a popular form that incorporated both spoken dialog as well as singing. Wolfgang Amadeus Mozart was a Freemason for much of his life and the Masonic connections to *The Magic Flute* have long been discussed by academics. However, beyond this, the opera is an incident-packed tale of the testing of true love. The overture featured here was the underlying theme in the episode of *Inspector Morse* entitled *Masonic Mysteries* where Morse was suspected of murdering a fellow singer in an amateur production of Mozart's opera.

9. **Beethoven** *Symphony No 5 in C Minor Opus 67 1st Movement Allegro con brio*
The opening to this symphony is, perhaps, one of the most famous of all in classical music. Beethoven started work on what would become Symphony No 5 in 1804 but it wasn't until December 22, 1808, that the completed work received its première in Vienna and was dedicated to his patrons Prince Franz Joseph von Lobkowitz and Count Razumovsky. The first movement featured here is in the traditional sonata form that Beethoven inherited from his predecessors, Haydn and Mozart (in which the main ideas that are introduced in the first few pages undergo elaborate development through many keys, with a dramatic return to the opening section about three-quarters of the way through). It starts out with two dramatic fortissimo phrases, the famous motif, commanding the listener's attention. Following the first four bars, Beethoven uses imitations and sequences to expand the theme, these pithy imitations tumbling over each other with such rhythmic regularity that they appear to form a single, flowing melody. Shortly after, a very short *fortissimo* bridge, played by the horns, takes place before a second theme is introduced. This second theme is in E flat major,

the relative major, and it is more lyrical, written *piano* and featuring the four-note motif in the string accompaniment. The codetta is again based on the four-note motif. The development section follows, using modulation, sequences and imitation, and including the bridge. During the recapitulation, there is a brief solo passage for oboe in quasi-improvisatory style, and the movement ends with a massive coda.

10. **Mendelssohn** *Violin Concerto in E Minor* Opus 64 3rd Movement Allegretto non troppo—Allegro motto vivace
One of the most popular and widely performed pieces of music for the violin, Opus 64 was the last major piece of orchestral music composed by Felix Mendelssohn. Originally proposed by Mendelssohn to his friend, Ferdinand David, in 1838, the piece was not to be completed for six years and eventually received its premiere in Leipzig on March 13, 1845, with David as soloist and Niels Gade, the Danish composer, as Conductor, due to Mendelssohn's illness. The composer conducted the piece for the first time on October 23, 1845. The concerto is in three movements, the third of which—Allegretto non troppo—Allegro motto vivace—is featured on the disc. A highly innovative piece of music, the concerto has influenced a number of later composers, including both Tchaikovsky and Sibelius. The noted violinist Joseph Joachim said in 1906, the year before his death, that "The Germans have four violin concertos. The greatest, most uncompromising is Beethoven's. The one by Brahms vies with it in seriousness. The richest, the most seductive, was written by Max Bruch. But the most inward, the heart's jewel, is Mendelssohn's."

11. **Brahms** *Ein deutches Requiem (A German Requiem)* Opus 45 4th Movement
In the mid-1860s, following the death of his mother in February 1865 and that of his mentor Robert Schumann a decade earlier, Johannes Brahms composed is single longest composition—*Ein deutches Requiem*. This large-scale choral work, sacred but non-liturgical, is unusual in that it is in German rather than Latin, with its text derived from the Lutheran Bible. Three movements of the requiem received

its première in December 1867, with all six movements being played together for the first time in Bremen Cathedral on April 10, 1868, with Brahms himself conducting. A further addition—a new fifth movement—was added subsequently. The text for the fourth movement was derived from Psalm 84 verses 1, 2 and 4.

12. **Wagner** *Die Walküre (The Valkyrie)*: Act III *Ritt der Walküren (Ride of the Valkyries)*
Richard Wagner was noted for his great and dramatic operas of which the four-part "Ring" cycle was perhaps his greatest triumph. *The Valkyrie* was the second of the operas to be completed and received its première in Munich on June 26, 1870. In the opera, the Ride begins in the prelude to the third act, building up successive layers of accompaniment until the curtain rises to reveal a mountain peak where four of the eight Valkyrie sisters—figures from Norse myth who elected those who were to die in battle—of Brünnhilde have gathered in preparation for the transportation of fallen heroes to Valhalla. As they are joined by the other four, the familiar tune is carried by the orchestra, while, above it, the Valkyries greet each other and sing their battle-cry. As a dramatic piece of music, the *Ride of the Valkyries* has been widely used in film, most notably during the helicopter attack on a Vietnamese village in *Apocalypse Now*.

13. **Tchaikovsky** *Swan Lake* Opus 20: finale
One of the leading composers of ballet music, Pyotr Ilyich Tchaikovsky was commissioned in May 1875 to write a new ballet, *Swan Lake*, by the Imperial Theatre. As a result of his financial condition he accepted the commission for what was to be his first ballet. Premièred in 1877, the work was an artistic failure, although musically it included some of the composer's most brilliantly orchestrated music. The version that we see and hear today is the result of revisions made in 1895, two years after the composer's death, by the noted choreographers Petipa and Ivanov. The ballet is in four acts. The first act witnesses the birthday party to mark the coming-of-age of Prince Siegfried. During the party a flight of swans appears. Act two sees Siegfried and his friends hunting swans by the lakeside. One swan, however, reveals to Siegfried that she is in fact a women, Odette,

changed into a swan by Rotbart. Back at the palace, Siegfried now has to select a wife. He selects Odile, Rotbart's daughter, in the mistaken belief that she is in fact Odette. Act four sees Odette condemned but Siegfried comes to the rescue and, defeating Rotbart in battle, breaks the spell and is reunited with Odette. The finale to the ballet, featured here, marks the final triumph of Siegfried and his reunion with Odette.

14. **Elgar** *Variations on an Original Theme ("Enigma")*
Opus 36: *IX Nimrod*
Sir Edward Elgar was perhaps the composer that best expressed the British Imperial ideal of the early 20th century. Probably Elgar's best-known orchestral composition, Opus 36—commonly called the *Enigma Variations*—was written in 1898 and 1899 before receiving its premiere at St James Hall, London, on June 19, 1899, where it was conducted by Hans Richter. The piece was dedicated to "my friends pictured within", as each variation was an affectionate portrayal of an individual from his family and friends. The ninth variation featured here portrayed Augustus J. Jaeger, a music editor at the London company of Novello & Co, who was both a close friend and advisor to Elgar. The German name Jäger translates into English as "hunter" and the titles is therefore a pun upon the name as Nimrod was a Patriarch in the Old Testament described as "a mighty hunter before the Lord". Subsequent to the première of the work, Elgar revealed that Jaeger had once visited him at a time of Elgar's life when the composer was depressed and to encourage him to persevere. Jaeger cited the example of Beethoven, and in particular the Piano Sonata No. 8 *Pathétique*, and as a result Elgar put a hint of the Beethoven piece into his own composition. The name of the entire work comes from Elgar who explained that the theme was a counterpoint to another larger name. However, he refused to identify this other theme, leading to much speculation as to what it might be. Given that the work celebrates friendship, a convincing case for *Auld Lang Syne* can be made. *Nimrod* as a piece is often used at funerals and is played annually at the Remembrance Day ceremony in November at the Cenotaph in London's Whitehall.

15. **Holst** *The Planets No. 4 Jupiter: The Bringer of Jollity*
The English composer Gustav Holst (1874-1934) was, for much of his career, known primarily as a composer of choral music. One piece, however, has ensured his presence amongst the greats of 20th century classical composition—*The Planets*—which received its première in 1918. Although much British classical music of the late 19th century had been characterized by insularity, *The Planets* demonstrates Holst's knowledge of and interest in musical trends in Europe, with the influence of Wagner, Ravel and Richard Strauss all evident. The suite consists of seven movements, all named after the planets in the solar system. *Suite No. 4, Jupiter: The Bringer of Jollity*, depicts the majesty of the largest of the planets whilst emphasizing an element of joviality. The central theme was later to be used by Holst for the setting of the hymn *I vow to thee my country*, as played at the wedding of HRH Prince Charles to Lady Diana Spencer.

FURTHER READING AND WEBSITES

The range of books and websites on classical music in general and on individual composers and pieces is vast. A small selection of both are detailed below. There is also a number of magazines devoted to the subject. It's worth noting that the *BBC Music Magazine* and *Classic fm* magazine normally come with a cover-mounted CD: these can represent a useful and cost-effective means of extending one's collection of classical music, both via the current issue and back issues, when available. CDs of classical music are widely available through high street stores, although the range available will inevitably vary according to the size of the shop. Online stores such as Amazon will also have stock of most recordings, as will the official websites of the major CD producers.

BOOKS

All Music Guide to Classical Music: The Definitive Guide to Classical Music; Chris Woodstar; Backbeat Books

Beethoven: His Life and Music; Jeremy Siepmann; Naxos Books

Chopin: His Life and Music; Jeremy Nicholas; Naxos Books

Classical Music for Dummies; Glenn Dicterow, David Pogue and Scott Speck; Hungry Minds Inc

Discover Early Music; Lucien Jenkins; Naxos Books

Discover Music of the 20th Century; David McCleery; Naxos Books

Discover Music of the Baroque Era; Clive Unger–Hamilton; Naxos Books

Discover Music of the Classical Era; Stephen Johnson; Naxos Books

Discover Music of the Romantic Era; David McCleery; Naxos Books

Dvorák: His Life and Music; Neil Wenborn; Naxos Books

Eyewitness Companions: Classical Music; edited by John Burrow; Dorling Kindersley

Haydn: His Life and Music; David Vickers; Naxos Books

Mahler: His Life and Music; Stephen Johnson; Naxos Books
Mendelssohn: His Life and Music; Neil Wenborn; Naxos Books

Mozart: His Life and Music; Jeremy Siepmann; Naxos Books

Penguin Guide to Recorded Classical Music; Ivan March, Edward Greenfield, Robert Layton and Paul Czajkowski; Penguin

Puccini: His Life and Music; Julian Haylock; Naxos Books

Rough Guide: Classical Music; edited by Joe Staines; Rough Guides

Rough Guide: Opera; edited by Matthew Boyden; Rough Guides

Tchaikovsky: His Life and Music; Jeremy Siepmann; Naxos Books

The Great Composers: The Lives and Music of the Great Classical Composers; Jeremy Nicholas

Wagner: His Life and Music; Stephen Johnson; Naxos Books

WEBSITES

bbc.co.uk: Official website for the British Broadcasting Corporation with links to BBC Radio Three and access to recent programmes via the BBC iPlayer

classicfm.co.uk: Official website of Classic fm
deccaclassics.com: British classical record label now controlled by Universal Music Group

deutschegrammophon.com: German classical record label now controlled by Universal Music Group

emirrecords.co.uk: One of the world's leading producers of recorded music with a large classical catalogue

en.wikipedia.org: Many of the pages relating to individual composers have extracts of their best-known pieces

harmoniamundi.com: French classical record label; website available in French, German, English and other languages

hyperion-records.co.uk: One of Britain's foremost producers of classical CDs; significant presence in the early music period; also releases the Helios range of budget CDs

naxos.com: Probably the primary producer of budget classical music CDs in the world

sonymusic.co.uk: One of the world's leading producers of recorded music with a large classical catalogue

There is also a number of websites devoted to music downloads from which classical music can be obtained. These include sites offering downloads commercially, including www.apple.com/uk/iTunes and www.napster.co.uk/Music_Download, and those that advertise free downloads, such as www.rawdownloads.com and www.ez-tracks.com.

GLOSSARY

Adagio–slow time (but faster than Largo)

Agitato–agitated or restless

Air–a tune. In the 16th century this was the English version of the Italian aria but with the development as opera as a distinctive musical form in the 17th century the word aria came to dominate this particular usage

Allegretto–diminutive of Allegro; used to indicate music slower than Allegro but quicker than Andante

Allegro–cheerful; historically used to indicate a lively or quick tune

Alto–the vocal part sung by women or boys with a low range

Anthem–a sacred vocal composition sung at Matins and Evensong in the Anglican Church; similar to the motet in Roman Catholicism, the anthem developed as an exclusively Anglican format after the Reformation

Antiphon–a response, usually sung in Gregorian chant, to a psalm or some other part of a religious service, such as at Vesper or at a Mass. This meaning gave rise to the "antiphony", a call-and-response style of singing

Aria–an air or song, generally used to refer to longer sings in oratorios and operas. Can also be used for sing–like instrumental movements

Arpeggio–notes sounded in chord

Andante–moderately slow time

Andantino–slightly quicker than Andante

Ballet–a sophisticated combination of music and dance performed on stage that developed from the late 16th century. Composers such as Tchaikovsky with, for example, *The Sleeping Beauty* and *Swan Lake*, composed music specifically for the ballet

Baritone–a male voice pitched between bass and tenor

Bass–a male voice sung at the lowest range

Cantata–a choral work; effectively a short oratoria or a lyric drama set to music but with no acting

Canticle–a hymn derived from text in the Bible, other than the Book of Psalms

Castrato–the high-pitched voice of a eunuch. The castration of singers was made illegal by Napoleon at the end of the 18th century although it was not until the late 19th century that the practice of castrating juvenile singers to prevent their voices breaking finally disappeared. The high-pitched voices were highly prized in eighteenth-century Italian operas and by the Catholic Church

Chamber Music–originally music designed for the private chamber rather than for the church or theater and therefore requiring fewer performers and more intimate in scale

Concerto–musical piece, usually of three movements, where a single core instrument (such as a piano) is backed by a full orchestra

Concerto grosso–similar to Concerto but where several core instruments are backed by an orchestra

Contralto–a woman's voice with a low range

Counterpoint–the art of combining melodies

Duet–a composition for two instrumentalists or singers

Falsetto–high–pitched notes sung by men who normally sing as Altos

Finale–the last movement of any composition

Forte–strong or loud

Fortissimo–very strong or loud

Galliard–a form of Renaissance dance and music that was popular across Europe in the 16th century

Grandioso–grandly

Grave–solemn and slow

Gregorian–plainsong church music associated with the Roman Catholic Church from the earliest days; largely superseded in the 16th century but rediscovered and popularized again from the early 20th century

Largo–slow time (slower than Adagio)

Larghetto–fairly slow time

Leader–the chief player amongst the first violins who, under the direction of the conductor, undertakes a number of roles, including rehearsal in the conductor's absence

Lento–slow

Libretto–a little book; now generally refers to the words of an oratorio or opera

Madrigal–a secular composition for two or more voices

Mass–a musical setting of the Ordinary of the Mass, comprising the Kyrie, Gloria in Excelsis, Credo, Sanctus and Agnus Dei

Mezzo soprano–a type of classical female singing voice in the range between soprano and contralto; mezzo is derived from the Italian world for middle or medium

Minuet–slow dance of French origin

Moderato–moderately

Motet–now regarded as an unaccompanied anthem used predominantly in Roman Catholic and Lutheran churches but originally an early form of polyphonic composition with words and music

Nonet–a musical composition for nine instruments

Obbligato–necessary or essential

Octet–a musical composition for eight instruments

Opera–drama where music, particularly singing, is essential

Operetta–a short opera or musical comedy

Oratoria–a musical composition, often sacred, where the singers and choir perform without costume and scenery

Overture–an instrumental prelude to an opera or ballet
Part song–a song for two or more voices

Pavan–a dance, of either Italian or Spanish origin, popular in the 16th and 17th centuries

Pianissimo–very softly

Piano–soft

Plainsong–general word for church music prior to the development of polyphony; largely dominated by Gregorian forms, although there were other styles

Pleno–full

Polka–a dance of Bohemian origin

Polonaise–a dance of Polish origin

Polska–a dance of Swedish origin

Polyphony–a style of music that combines two or more tunes in harmony

Prelude–a piece of music used as an introduction to a longer composition

Prestissimo–very quickly

Presto–fast

Quartet–a musical composition for four instruments or voices

Quintet–a musical composition for five instruments or voices

Requiem–a mass for the dead, comprising Introit, Kyrie, Gradual and Tract, Dies Irae, Offertory, Sanctus, Benedictus, Agnus Dei and Lux Aeterna

Sextet–a musical composition for six instruments or voices

Sonata–an extended musical composition for one or two instruments

Soprano–a woman's voice with a high range

Stabat Mater–a hymn about the crucifixion, sung during the week prior to Easter

Suite–an extended composition for one or two instruments or full orchestra, with a number of movements in dance form

Symphony–a longer musical composition formed of a number of distinct movements

Tango–a dance of Mexican origin

Tempo–time

Tenor–vocal, part sung by men with a high range

Treble–vocal, part sung by women and boys with a high range before their voices break

Trio–a musical composition for three instruments or voices

Vivace–lively

Voluntary–a composition, usually for an organ, played at a church service

Waltz–a type of dance, increasingly popular in the 19th century, of German origin

PHOTO CREDITS

INDEX